War Aga
Depres

Pragmatic Approaches to Get Back on Track from Life's Fluctuations and

Restore Emotional Equilibrium After Life's Ups and Downs

Adegboye S. Aduragbemi

INTRODUCTION

Facing Life's Unexpected Storms: Understanding Situational Depression

Life is unpredictable, as anything may happen in life. On one hand, it can fill us with happiness, enthusiasm, and achievement; on the other, it might crush us with unforeseen difficulties, tragedy, or mental turmoil. Intense emotional reactions, brought on by these trying times, can make it seem like we are drowning beneath an impossible weight. Many people experience Situational Depression when the stresses of life get too severe. This disorder is more widespread than most people think, and it is frequently misunderstood or downplayed.

Distinguishing between clinical depression and situational depression, or "Adjustment Disorder with Depressed Mood," is essential. It is an intense yet fleeting emotional reaction to traumatic experiences in life. This type of depression can significantly affect a person's capacity to carry out daily tasks, and it can be brought on by a variety of stressful life events, such as the loss of a loved one, a job, a divorce, money problems, or other significant changes. Although the intensity of the sensations of melancholy, worry, and despair is comparable to that of clinical depression, the origins of these emotions lie in certain life events.

If you or someone you know struggles through tough times and feels helpless in the face of events beyond your control, you may find this book helpful. Here, you can find information about situational depression, its causes, and, most importantly, steps to take to recover and advance your life.

Justification for Addressing Situational Depression

"Tough it out" and "get over it" are phrases that persons with situational depression hear far too frequently. When people regard depression as a normal reaction to bad things happening in life, they may try to minimize its importance. Still, situational depression is a genuine emotional illness that calls for empathy and support. When you're overwhelmed with sadness, worry, or trauma, it might be hard to see past your current situation and go forward. This book attempts to acknowledge and help readers get through those emotions.

A lack of strength does not indicate situational depression. Faced with life's numerous obstacles, it's a natural reaction. However, it can cause a downward spiral into a more severe emotional state or even more severe mental health problems if appropriate coping skills are not in place. That is why it is critical to comprehend it and deal with it promptly.

In this lesson on "Understanding and Overcoming Situational Depression," we will go over the following aspects of Frequently Asked Questions (FAQs):

- **How Situational Depression Works:** To begin with, how does situational depression compare to other types of depression? To assist you in recognizing it in yourself or others, we will explain the symptoms, causes, and triggers.

- **How Life Changes Affect Us Emotionally:** We will look at the most typical causes of this kind of sadness and how they can feel so overpowering, including but not limited to losing a job, a relationship, relocating to a new place, or losing a loved one. Learn practical approaches to regulating your emotions during challenging circumstances, such as mindfulness, stress-reduction exercises, and ways to build resilience. Coping strategies and self-care are also essential.

- **Consulting an Expert:** At times, methods of self-help alone are inadequate. This article will discuss the signs that it is time to reach out for help and how medications, therapy, or counselling can aid in the healing process.

- **Keeping Hope Alive:** This book will show you that depression is just a phase that will pass. Even in the face of overwhelming adversity, there is hope for recovery, development, and strength.

You Have Companions

Feeling alone in your battle is a very alienating part of situational depression. No, you're not. Millions of people annually are impacted by situational depression. Anyone dealing with significant life stresses can be affected, regardless of age, gender, or background. There is hope at the end of the darkest times, and this book will show you how to find it by sharing insights, true tales, and professional counsel.

The fact that you or a loved one has chosen to read this book suggests that you are experiencing difficulty. The first step towards understanding and healing is already within you, whether amid an emotional storm or just getting ready for life's inevitable obstacles.

The Path Forward

There is no easy way to deal with the intense emotions accompanying significant life changes or losses, and navigating life's challenges is never easy. You may recover your equilibrium and health with the correct resources, encouragement, and attitude. With any luck, you'll find some solace and helpful advice in this book while you work to overcome situational depression. Along this path, you will discover that tough times are inevitable but that you are resilient enough to overcome adversity and become stronger.

Chapter One

Conquering Situational Depression: The Narrative of Emma

Emma has consistently exhibited a cheerful and motivated disposition. She thrived in her profession, maintained a tight-knit group of friends, and was in a nurturing relationship. However, when her company saw an abrupt downsizing, she was unceremoniously terminated after years of diligent effort. The astonishment was profound. Experiencing job loss resembled the forfeiture of a segment of her identity. The issue extended beyond financial insecurity; it encompassed a profound sense of failure and ambiguity regarding her future.

Initially, Emma was confident in her ability to manage the situation. She reassured herself that it was merely an obstacle. However, as the weeks progressed into months, her self-doubt and anxiety intensified. She experienced a sense of disconnection from her pals and progressively retreated from social engagements. Her urge to seek new employment dissipated, and she started to grapple with fundamental everyday tasks. The previously bright and enthusiastic individual appeared remote, supplanted by someone who felt adrift and burdened by sorrow.

Her boyfriend observed the alteration, but Emma dismissed the concerns, attributing it to the stress of job searching. Emma was unaware that she had succumbed to **situational depression**, prompted by her job loss and the ambiguity surrounding her future. It was not clinical depression, yet it profoundly impacted her life. She ceased socializing, experienced persistent weariness, and felt incapable of seizing chances that arose.

Emma engaged in an extensive conversation with her companion after missing another significant social function due to her inability to summon the energy to go. They indicated that this was no longer merely a "bad mood"—it was something more profound. Realizing that her emotions were not dissipating independently, Emma pursued assistance.

The Crucial Juncture

Emma commenced therapy with a counsellor specializing in adjustment disorders, encompassing situational depression. For the first time, she could discuss the emotional impact of her job loss candidly. Her counsellor emphasized that situational sadness is a normal response to substantial life alterations, and it is acceptable to experience feelings of being overwhelmed. This validation constituted the initial phase of her therapeutic journey.

They collaborated on techniques to regulate her stress and emotional reactions. Emma acquired knowledge of cognitive behavioural therapy (CBT) strategies to confront the detrimental ideas that had impeded her progress. Rather than perceiving her job loss as a failure, she started reframing the circumstance—viewing it as an opportunity to reevaluate her career and personal aspirations.

Emma additionally integrated self-care into her regimen. She commenced documenting her emotions, which facilitated the release of her tensions. She allocated time for physical exercise, which she had previously overlooked, and discovered it enhanced her mood. Emma commenced practising mindfulness meditation, which assisted her in managing anxiety and remaining anchored in the now rather than perpetually fretting about the future.

Progressing Ahead

In the ensuing months, Emma gradually restored her feeling of purpose. Despite the challenging labour market, she engaged in freelance work, giving her a sense of autonomy and restoring her confidence. She re-established connections with friends and candidly shared her challenges, fortifying her relationships and enhancing her support.

Emma had secured a new position by year-end, rekindling her enthusiasm for her profession. The path to recovery was not linear; it involved setbacks and challenging days, but she acquired the skills to regulate her emotions and navigate life's unpredictabilities. Significantly, she recognized that situational depression, although distressing, is a transient condition that can be surmounted with appropriate support and techniques.

Contemplation

Upon reflection, Emma recognized that her job loss had constituted a pivotal moment in her life, impacting her professionally and emotionally. It compelled her to confront her anxieties, pursue assistance, and cultivate resilience. What was initially perceived as a conclusion transformed into the inception of a new chapter, and she emerged from the experience more resilient, self-aware, and adept at confronting life's problems.

Emma's narrative exemplifies that although situational melancholy may seem overwhelming, it is surmountable. With appropriate tools, support, and self-compassion, individuals can effectively traverse life's most formidable obstacles and emerge with enhanced strength and perspective.

A Narrative of Adversity: David's Conflict with Situational Depression

David was a man who consistently took pride in his strength and dependability. From inception, he established a prosperous enterprise and garnered respect within his community for his diligence and tenacity. He was wed to his high school sweetheart, Laura, and they had two offspring together. Life appeared stable and favourable until an unforeseen turn of events altered everything.

David's company declared bankruptcy due to unexpected market fluctuations and several poor business mistakes. The failure of his enterprise was not merely a monetary setback; it adversely affected his sense of identity and self-esteem. The company represented his life's work, into which he had invested years of effort; witnessing its disintegration made him feel like he had failed himself and his family and employees.

Initially, David believed he could recover. He resolved to persevere through the difficulties and identify a solution. However, weeks transformed into months, and David commenced a descent into profound depression. The burden of his failure, financial strain, and the obligation to maintain his family culminated in an overwhelming emotional distress that he found difficult to cope with.

The Onset of Situational Depression

Initially, David strove to maintain composure. He kept a courageous facade for his family, although emotionally, he was disintegrating. He became disheartened in his search for new employment, believing he could not restore what he had lost. Minor failures, which may include rejection from a prospective company or witnessing the success of former coworkers, seemed devastating. The formerly self-assured and motivated individual transformed into someone who hardly ventured outside.

David started to isolate himself from his family, experiencing humiliation over his perceived failure. His marriage began to deteriorate as he withdrew from Laura and the children. Laura observed the transformation in him and attempted to persuade him to seek assistance, but David dismissed her, convinced that it required neither therapy nor sympathy. He believed he could manage alone, unaware he was descending further into situational melancholy. David was unprepared for the despair induced by the immense stress of losing his business and sense of identity. He lacked the mental resources to manage the abrupt disruption in his life, and instead of seeking assistance, he further withdrew into isolation.

The Absence of Support and Deterioration

Over time, David's mental health declined. He commenced self-medication with booze, anticipating it would alleviate the anguish and assist him in forgetting the escalating sense of failure he bore daily. The consumption of alcohol, however, exacerbated his emotional condition, amplifying his sense of despair. He grew increasingly irritated and aloof, directing his anger at Laura during disputes and becoming emotionally inaccessible to his children. Friends expressed concern for his well-being, although David declined to disclose his feelings. He believed that acknowledging his difficulties would merely validate his perception of failure. He sought to avoid being perceived as weak or incompetent in managing his issues. Eventually, individuals ceased their attempts to contact him. Even Laura, who cherished him profoundly, struggled to connect with him and felt powerless as she witnessed his decline.

The Critical Juncture

David's denial of his depression and reluctance to seek assistance ultimately resulted in catastrophic outcomes. The pressure on his marriage became intolerable. Laura, unable to connect with him emotionally and exhausted from attempting to assist someone who rejected support, resolved to relocate with the children temporarily. It constituted a final endeavour to demonstrate to David that circumstances had escalated to a critical juncture, hoping that it would compel him to acknowledge the severity of his issue.

Rather than acting as a wake-up call, David's sense of failure was exacerbated. The temporary loss of his family constituted the ultimate setback. He now felt utterly isolated and forsaken, unable to perceive any escape from the predicament he faced. Instead of utilizing this opportunity to pursue therapy or connect with his support network, David descended more into alcohol and loneliness.

The Consequences

David's narrative is a lamentable one. His inability to recognise or accept assistance for his situational melancholy finally resulted in his demise. Although his company loss was distressing, it was a challenge he could have surmounted with time, help, and an appropriate mindset. His reluctance to confront his emotional challenges and his pride in managing matters independently hindered him from obtaining the necessary assistance.

His marriage concluded in divorce, as Laura could no longer endure witnessing the man she loved decline without any inclination to change. She sought to shield her children from the escalating instability in their household. After years of supporting David, she recognized that his unwillingness to seek assistance was beyond her influence.

David was unable to recuperate. Devoid of familial support and having estranged his friends, he persisted on a trajectory of self-destruction. His situational sadness, initially a transient phase, evolved into a defining characteristic of his existence. The demise of his enterprise precipitated a series of subsequent losses stemming from his inability to confront emotional difficulties directly and his refusal to recognise his need for assistance.

Insights from David's Narrative

David's narrative serves as a poignant warning that situational sadness, although sometimes transient, can yield catastrophic long-term repercussions if neglected. The emotional consequences of life alterations, such as unemployment, financial difficulties, or significant upheavals, can result in profound feelings of hopelessness and despair. Situational depression need not be permanent; it can be managed, and recovery is attainable.

David's inability to transcend his sadness was not due to the insurmountability of his circumstances. His failure to seek assistance was the reason. He withdrew when he required companionship. He resorted to maladaptive coping strategies rather than seeking support from his family, friends, or a professional.

David's narrative acts as a cautionary tale for anyone grappling with situational depression. It is essential to identify the indicators, confront the mental distress, and get the necessary help to progress. Situational depression does not define an individual's existence, but one's response to it can influence their destiny.

Chapter Two

The Basic FAQs About Situational Depression

Could you please explain the difference between clinical depression and situational depression?

Situational depression, also known as adjustment disorder with low mood, is an emotional response to a particular stressor or life event that lasts for a brief period. Situational depression is distinct from clinical depression since it is associated with specific events, like significant life changes, tragedies, or losses. Sadness, hopelessness, and a lack of interest are symptoms that may be similar to clinical depression; however, after the stressor is dealt with or the person adjusts to the circumstance, the symptoms of situational depression usually go away.

For many people, what kinds of stressful situations can catalyze developing situational depression?

Issues in relationships, money, employment, school, moving, illness, grief, or trauma are among the many stresses and life events that can set off situational depression. A person's perception of stability can be disrupted, and these stressors intensify their feelings of grief, anxiety, and distress.

19

What is the usual duration of situational depression?

Symptoms of situational depression usually disappear within six months after the beginning of the stressful event or stressor that initially triggered them. When people with situational depression learn to adapt, reach out for help, or deal with the source of their stress, they often find that their symptoms begin to improve.

Could you tell me what signs of situational depression look like?

If you are looking for a list of symptoms associated with situational depression, here they are changes in appetite or weight, sleep disturbances, low energy or exhaustion, trouble concentrating, feelings of guilt or worthlessness, irritability, and withdrawal from usual activities or social interactions. While these symptoms might not be as severe as those of clinical depression, they can nevertheless have a significant influence on how effectively you operate day-to-day.

How does one go about diagnosing situational depression?

For a mental health expert to identify situational depression, they need to go over the patient's symptoms, medical history, and whether or not there has been a recent stressful event in their lives. To get to the bottom of the symptoms, the doctor may need to rule out other possible mental health issues. When the symptoms are directly linked to a specific stressor and do not fit the criteria for another mental condition, a diagnosis of adjustment disorder with depressed mood is usually made.

When dealing with situational depression, what methods have proven to be effective?

To treat situational depression, doctors usually recommend looking at the root cause of the patient's distress, giving them tools to deal with the stress, and encouraging them to develop more adaptive ways of coping. Cognitive behavioural therapy (CBT), relaxation techniques, stress management strategies, social support networks, and individual or group therapy may all be part of this. Medications can help with symptoms like anxiety and sleep problems in some people. The purpose of therapy is to assist the patient in making sense of their circumstance and getting back on their feet emotionally.

If untreated, may situational depression progress to clinical depression?

Although situational depression is usually thought of as a transient disorder, it can progress to clinical depression if not addressed or if the root cause of the stress continues. Seek expert assistance for assessment and therapy if situational depression symptoms persist beyond the anticipated duration or intensify with time. It is possible to lessen the severity and duration of a depressive condition by taking action against situational depression when it is still in its early stages.

How can people recognise when their emotions are just standard and when they are suffering from situational depression?

It might be difficult to tell the difference between situational depression and normal emotional reactions to life events. It is expected to feel sad, stressed, or grieve when faced with adversity, but situational depression is characterized by intense emotions that last for a long time and make it hard to function or enjoy life. An examination by a mental health expert is necessary if feelings of sadness last longer than usual or if they impact one's ability to go about one's everyday life, one's relationships, or one's general health.

How can one take care of themselves to cope with situational depression?

Taking care of oneself can be helpful when dealing with situational depression. Some examples of this include getting enough sleep, eating well, exercising regularly, and using relaxing methods like meditation or mindfulness. Other helpful things that must be done include doing things you enjoy, hanging out with people who have your back, making reasonable plans, and getting help from experts when you need it. It is recommended to take proactive measures to address the root cause of stress or consult a mental health expert to aid in recovery and resilience.

Is it a reflection of inadequacy or failure on my part to experience situational depression?

No, being depressed due to a particular circumstance is not an indication of being weak or failing as an individual. It is a natural reaction to difficult situations or stresses in life and can impact everyone, regardless of their strength. Bravery and proactive coping mechanisms are on display when someone seeks assistance for situational depression. You must acknowledge your honest sentiments and get your help to survive challenging circumstances.

Is it possible for kids and teens to experience situational depression?

Children and teenagers are not the only age groups that might be impacted by situational depression. When kids and teens have difficulties at home, in the classroom, in social situations, or as a result of trauma, they may develop situational depression. If they want to assist young people in dealing with stress and build resilience, parents, teachers, and other caretakers must pay close attention to any changes in behaviour, mood, or academic performance and offer the proper support and direction. It is possible to stop situational depression from becoming a significant mental health crisis by intervening early.

Can one avoid experiencing situational depression?

Although absolute prevention of situational depression may not always be achievable, there are measures that people may take to lessen their vulnerability and strengthen their ability to cope with adversity. These include learning effective ways to deal with stressful situations, surrounding oneself with supportive people, regularly exercising these skills, and getting professional assistance when necessary. Resilience and mental health can also be enhanced by increasing self-awareness, recognizing the early warning signs of discomfort, and actively working to alleviate stress.

What can loved ones do to help a friend or family member who is suffering from situational depression?

When someone is going through situational depression, having someone to talk to, someone to understand, and someone to validate their feelings can be a great help. Companionship, social engagement, practical help with daily duties, and encouragement to seek expert help are all helpful. Being present and supportive when needed is as important as respecting the individual's limits and autonomy.

Whereas grief and sorrow are similar, is situational depression?

Both situational depression and grief/mourning are emotional responses to significant life changes or losses; therefore, the question is comparable but not exhaustive. Grief and loss are only two examples of the many stresses that can trigger situational depression; other common triggers include relationship issues, career changes, and financial troubles. Although it's normal to feel sad after losing something important in your life, if your symptoms of situational depression are severe or ongoing, you may need to see a doctor.

Can other mental health issues coexist with situational depression?

Yes, additional mental health disorders, including anxiety disorders, PTSD, or substance use disorders, can co-occur with situational depression. Having to deal with more than one mental health issue at once can make diagnosis and treatment more complex. It may necessitate a holistic strategy that considers each illness's specific requirements. A thorough examination and integrated therapy from experienced professionals are necessary for those experiencing situational depression alongside other mental health concerns.

What can I do if I think I may be suffering from situational depression or if I know someone who may be?

Seek the assistance of a trained mental health expert without delay if you or a loved one exhibits any of the symptoms of situational depression. It may be necessary to consult a psychiatrist, therapist, counsellor, or primary care physician to get an accurate diagnosis and treatment plan. Furthermore, seeking reliable people for emotional support and encouragement, such as family, friends, or support groups, might be helpful when situations get tough. An individual's health, happiness, and ability to deal with adversity can all benefit from taking preventative measures against situational depression.

One of the symptoms of adjustment disorder is a gloomy mood; what are the causes of situational depression?

Significant life changes or stresses, which include marital issues, job loss, money troubles, academic pressures, moving, being sick, or losing a loved one, are what set off situational depression, which is also known as adjustment disorder with low mood. Negativity, pessimism, and despair are emotional responses that might result when these stresses shake up a person's sense of stability.

What factors in a person's life can lead to the onset of situational depression?

Situational depression can develop when adverse life experiences test a person's coping mechanisms, resilience, and adaptability. Divorce, losing a job, or experiencing trauma are all events that can shake a person's feeling of stability and control, which can cause them to feel emotionally distressed and even depressed. Situational depression can grow and become more severe depending on the person's coping abilities, support system, and the length and severity of the stressor.

How can situational depression impact one's ability to go about their regular life?

People with situational depression may find it very difficult to go about their everyday lives and enjoy the things that are important to them. Some of the most common side effects include being sad, not wanting to do anything, having trouble focusing, being irritable, and withdrawing from social engagements. It might be challenging to carry out duties and enjoy fun activities while these symptoms impact one's employment, relationships, and general health.

Are there any effects on physical health from situational depression?

Yes, situational depression can have a variety of effects on physical health. The immune system can be weakened, inflammation can be amplified, and physical health issues like diabetes, chronic pain, and cardiovascular disease can be either precipitated or worsened by persistent stress and depression. There may be further effects on physical health and general functioning from changes in hunger, sleep disruptions, and reduced self-care.

What role do social support systems and connections have in the development of situational depression?

Relationships and social support greatly influence the development and management of situational depression. By validating and understanding one's emotions and providing practical support, positive social support can mitigate the adverse effects of stressors. On the other side, situational depression symptoms could be worsened by strained relationships or a lack of support, which can increase feelings of loneliness, isolation, and discomfort.

Can situational depression progress to other forms of mental illness if left untreated?

Although situational depression is usually seen as a temporary response to specific stresses, it can lead to other mental health issues, including major depressive disorder or anxiety disorders, if left untreated or for an extended period. Increased susceptibility to more severe and long-lasting mental health problems may result from the effects of stress and unresolved emotional difficulties on brain chemistry, mood regulation, and coping strategies. Early intervention and healthy coping mechanisms are essential to lessen the impact of this risk.

What effects can situational depression have on performance in the workplace or the classroom?

Because it hinders focus, motivation, and productivity, situational depression can have a significant influence on how well a person does in school or on the job. People may struggle to concentrate, complete assignments on time, or function at their typical level. Symptoms like lethargy, indifference, or trouble juggling tasks might lead to absenteeism, poor performance at work, or unsatisfactory GPA. It is necessary to deal with the root causes of stress and put supportive measures in place to lessen their impact.

When it comes to managing and preventing situational depression, how important is coping style?

One's coping style can have an impact on how situational depression is developed and handled. Adaptive coping mechanisms, which may include reaching out to others for support, finding creative solutions to problems, and viewing challenges through a positive lens, may help people deal with stressful situations and lessen the toll that hardship takes on their mental health. On the other hand, negative ways of coping with stress, such as avoiding problems, dwelling on negative thoughts, or abusing substances, can make things worse and prolong the symptoms of situational depression.

How can situational depression impact one's sense of self-worth and self-esteem?

People with situational depression may experience a decline in their sense of self-worth and self-esteem as a result of their negative self-perceptions. Negative self-evaluations and beliefs can erode self-confidence and self-esteem when despair, hopelessness, or failure persist. Failing to handle stressful situations or live up to one's expectations can also fuel the fire of inadequacy and self-doubt. One way to combat these consequences is to cultivate resilience and self-compassion by surrounding oneself with supportive people and learning healthy coping mechanisms.

What happens when situational depression is untreated in the long run?

The mental, emotional, and physical health of an individual might be negatively impacted in the long run if situational depression goes untreated. Severe mental health disorders, such as major depressive disorder, post-traumatic stress disorder, or generalized anxiety disorder, may be more likely to develop in those who experience prolonged discomfort and chronic stress. Problems in interpersonal relationships, performance in the workplace or school, and general well-being can result from untreated situational depression. The best way to avoid these long-term effects of situational depression is to treat it early on with the right treatments and support.

How can situational depression impact relationships and family dynamics?

Yes, family dynamics and relationships can be impacted by situational depression. It can interrupt communication, increase tension, and strain interpersonal bonds. People who are depressed due to a particular scenario may act irritably and moodily, have trouble carrying out their duties and obligations, or isolate themselves from family and friends. Conflicts or misunderstandings may arise when family members react with stress and frustration to the symptoms experienced by the affected individual. A person's ability to cope and bounce back from adversity can be enhanced by honest dialogue, understanding, and the encouragement of loved ones.

What effects does situational depression have on the capacity to make decisions and solve problems?

Decreased motivation, clarity of mind, and cognitive flexibility might make it harder to make decisions and solve problems when dealing with situational depression. Some people have trouble thinking critically, foreseeing potential outcomes, or finding workable solutions. Further impediments to decision-making and intensifying feelings of overwhelm and hesitation can be self-doubt, negative thought patterns, and ruminating. You can lessen the impact on your brain by caring for yourself and reaching out to people you trust for support.

Is it only a transient ailment, situational depression?

It is often believed that situational depression is a transient condition and that symptoms will go away after the source of stress or life event is dealt with or adjusted to. A person's coping mechanisms, social support system, and the specifics of the stressor all have a role in how long and how bad situational depression lasts. Untreated situational depression might cause further long-term mental health issues or last longer than anticipated in certain people.

Do happy life events have the potential to trigger situational depression?

Although situational depression is more often linked to stressful or adverse life events, it can also happen when there are positive changes or transitions in one's life. Feelings of overload or stress can arise due to adjustment difficulties and conflicting emotions brought on by life changes like marriage, moving, getting a promotion at work, or becoming a parent. Emotional reactions to life events are complicated, as this syndrome, which is sometimes called "adjustment disorder with depressed mood," demonstrates.

To what extent do people's cultural and social backgrounds impact their likelihood of suffering from situational depression?

Cultural or socioeconomic elements can significantly impact the manifestation and impact of situational depression. The stigma, attitudes, and cultural norms that surround mental health issues might influence whether people are willing to seek assistance, talk about their symptoms, or get the treatment they need. Some people may be more susceptible to stress and have fewer coping mechanisms in place due to socioeconomic status, prejudice, or lack of resources. Supporting individuals with situational depression in a culturally competent and inclusive manner requires acknowledging and addressing societal and cultural influences.

Can one avoid experiencing situational depression?

Although it might not be able to avoid situational depression altogether, there are measures to lessen the likelihood of it happening and lessen its severity when it does. These include learning effective ways to deal with stressful situations, surrounding oneself with supportive people, regularly exercising these skills, and getting professional assistance when necessary. Individuals can improve their capacity to handle life's difficulties and reduce the likelihood of situational depression by developing resilience via self-awareness, problem-solving abilities, and adaptive coping mechanisms.

Does gender have a role in how situational sadness is felt and shown?

Studies have shown that different genders are more prone to specific types of stress, including interpersonal disputes and caregiving duties, which can contribute to the development and manifestation of situational depression. Furthermore, gender roles and societal expectations might influence how people deal with stress, whether they seek help, and how easily they are affected by certain types of stress. Recognizing that people of both sexes can experience situational depression and offering solutions that are accessible to all is critical for meeting the mental health needs of our community.

Chapter Three

Causes of situational depression (an adjustment disorder characterized by a low mood)

How often do you see specific symptoms that could indicate the onset of situational depression?

Dealing with significant life changes or stresses, like marital issues, money troubles, job loss, academic pressure, illness, or the death of a loved one, is a common risk factor for situational depression. Some people may be more vulnerable because they have fewer tools for dealing with stress, have less social support, have experienced trauma or ACEs in the past, or have a history of mental health issues.

To what extent are stressful events, both short and long-term, associated with an increased likelihood of developing situational depression?

Developing situational depression is heavily influenced by the severity and length of stressful events. People are more likely to have depressive symptoms after being exposed to chronic stress or numerous stressors over an extended period since these situations might overwhelm their resistance and coping systems. Trauma and other forms of unexpected, severe loss can have far-reaching effects on mental health and raise the likelihood of developing situational depression.

Does situational sadness tend to manifest itself more frequently during specific life transitions?

Divorce, losing a job, moving, retiring, or becoming a parent are all life changes and obstacles that might increase the risk of situational depression. A person may experience emotional pain and adjustment issues as a result of these changes because they shake their feeling of security, identity, or purpose. Furthermore, situational depression is more likely to develop during transitions that include substantial changes in role or increased responsibility, both of which can increase stress levels.

How does the likelihood of situational depression vary among individuals based on their coping style?

The risk of situational depression might vary from person to person based on their coping style. An individual's vulnerability to the onset of depressive symptoms can be mitigated by the use of adaptive coping mechanisms, such as reaching out to others for support, finding creative solutions to problems, and viewing things in a positive light. Stress and situational depression can worsen when people resort to unhealthy coping mechanisms like substance abuse, rumination, or avoidance.

Is it possible for elements related to biology or genetics to increase the likelihood of acquiring situational depression?

While external stresses are the most common cause of situational depression, a person's susceptibility to the disorder may also be influenced by their genetic makeup and biological makeup. An individual's stress threshold, ability to regulate their mood, and the likelihood of developing depression in reaction to stressful life experiences may be impacted by specific genetic variants or predispositions, according to research. An individual's susceptibility to situational depression may be influenced by neurobiological factors, such as changes in brain chemistry or functioning, which in turn affect the stress response.

Are people more likely to experience situational depression if they have a history of mental health issues?

People who already have anxiety disorders, PTSD, or a history of depression may be more likely to experience situational depression when faced with new challenges or changes in their lives. When faced with adversity, people with these illnesses may be more susceptible to emotional distress, have less effective coping mechanisms, and be more likely to experience depressive symptoms. During difficult times, those with previous mental health issues must receive the help they need.

What is the relationship between a person's risk of situational depression and their history of trauma or adverse childhood experiences?

The likelihood of suffering from situational depression in adulthood is significantly impacted by a history of trauma or adverse childhood experiences (ACEs). Adverse childhood experiences, such as abuse, neglect, or disruption in the family, can have long-lasting effects on a person's capacity to regulate their emotions, form healthy attachments, and cope with stress and depression as they grow older. Situational depression can develop in those who have experienced adverse childhood experiences (ACEs), which can lead to heightened emotional reactivity, trouble building trustworthy relationships, and maladaptive coping mechanisms.

Do certain demographic variables influence the likelihood of developing situational depression?

A person's age, gender, financial position, and cultural background are some of the demographic variables that can impact their risk of developing situational depression. Some people's stresses are specific to their age, such as the pressures of school or work, while others are more general, such as the realities of ageing, retirement, or health issues. Hormonal changes, cultural norms, and social expectations may put women at a higher risk. Individuals' vulnerability to stresses and their capacity to manage are influenced by socioeconomic disparities, discrimination, and access to resources, which in turn affect the likelihood of situational depression.

Does the presence or absence of social support influence the likelihood of developing situational depression?

The importance of social support in reducing the likelihood of situational depression cannot be overstated. It is essential to have social support from people you know and trust to cope with stress and become more resilient. This support can come from emotional validation, practical help, and a feeling of belonging. On the flip side, situational depression can be worsened by a lack of social support or damaged relationships, which can make it harder to solve problems or control emotions, make people feel even more alone, and rob them of essential coping tools.

Does one's character have any bearing on the likelihood of developing situational depression?

Specific personality features may impact the likelihood of developing situational depression. As an example, people who score higher on the neuroticism or negative emotionality scale may find it harder to control their emotions and are more likely to suffer from situational depression when faced with stressful situations. On the other side, characteristics like optimism, resilience, and adaptive coping mechanisms can lessen the severity of stress and guard against the onset of depression.

What role do cultural prejudice and discrimination have in increasing the likelihood of situational depression?

People's attitudes and beliefs about mental health and cultural stigma can impact their desire to seek help, report symptoms, or get the treatment they need for situational depression. Individuals' susceptibility to situational depression may be influenced by cultural ideas, norms, and expectations related to mental health, which in turn influence how people perceive stress, how they cope with it, and whether or not they seek treatment. Improving access to care and meeting mental health needs requires eliminating cultural stigma, increasing mental health literacy, and establishing culturally competent support systems.

Is the likelihood of developing situational depression influenced by external factors?

The risk of situational depression can be increased when people's sense of safety, security, and stability is disrupted by environmental stressors such as exposure to violence, natural catastrophes, community turmoil, or environmental risks. Some people may find that these stresses are too much to handle, and others may experience traumatic reactions or even depression as a result. Disparities in housing stability, healthcare access, and socioeconomic status can also affect people's vulnerability to stress and coping mechanisms, which in turn might affect the likelihood of developing situational depression.

Is there any evidence that physical ailments or chronic health problems increase the likelihood of developing situational depression?

Yes, people are more likely to experience situational depression if they are dealing with long-term health issues or physical disorders that cause them a great deal of hardship. Coping with symptoms, making lifestyle changes, and enduring medical treatment for long-term health concerns can all contribute to mental anguish and adjustment challenges. Another factor that can increase the likelihood of developing situational depression is the effect that physical sickness has on everyday functioning, independence, and quality of life. These factors can lead to feelings of helplessness, frustration, or melancholy.

The likelihood of developing situational depression: how is it influenced by substance misuse or dependence?

Because it worsens stress, hinders coping strategies, and disrupts emotional regulation, substance misuse or dependency can raise the likelihood of situational depression. As a harmful coping mechanism, substance abuse can help people avoid or lessen the impact of stressful situations and dull, unpleasant emotions or alleviate symptoms of mental illness. Substance misuse, on the other hand, can make depression symptoms worse, make it harder to solve problems effectively, and even cause situational depression. It is crucial to address these concerns through thorough treatment and support To lessen the likelihood of depression occurring at the same time as substance use disorders.

Do you know of any drugs or therapies that might make you more likely to experience situational depression?

Some medications or medical treatments may increase the risk of situational depression due to their effects on physiological or neurological functioning or as a side effect. Some chronic disease drugs, hormone treatments, and corticosteroids, for instance, can influence energy levels, cognitive functioning, and mood control, all of which may amplify the symptoms of depression. Medical procedures, like chemotherapy or surgery, can add stress and uncertainty to an already difficult time, making patients more susceptible to situational melancholy.

Is it possible for unforeseen circumstances, like problems with money or the law, to increase the likelihood of developing situational depression?

Yes, significant life changes, such as dealing with the law, money woes, or a dramatic shift in one's socioeconomic position, can add stress and difficulty to one's life, increasing the likelihood of developing situational depression. Problems with the law, such as court cases, criminal accusations, or jail time, can cause people to feel helpless, humiliated, or hopeless. Similar to how debt, unemployment, or housing instability can lead to ongoing stresses, low self-esteem, and an increased risk of situational depression, so can other financial issues. It is crucial to address underlying stresses and get the help you need to manage the mental health effects of these life events.

The symptoms and diagnosis of situational depression

Could you please explain the difference between clinical depression and situational depression?

Situational depression, sometimes called adjustment disorder with depressed mood, is a mental illness in which a person experiences a worsening of their mood symptoms in reaction to specific stressful events or changes in their lives. When faced with or adjusted to a stressful occurrence, situational depression usually goes away, in contrast to clinical depression, which can be more long-lasting and unconnected to any particular cause.

To make a diagnosis of situational depression, what are the most typical symptoms?

Feelings of worthlessness or guilt, changes in appetite or weight, sleep disturbances, exhaustion or lack of energy, trouble concentrating or making decisions, thoughts of death or suicide, and persistent sadness, hopelessness, or despair are common symptoms of situational depression. These symptoms usually appear within three months of a stressful event and severely limit daily functioning.

Mental health providers, how do they identify a case of situational depression?

Assessing the patient's symptoms, medical history, and current life circumstances allows mental health experts to identify situational depression. The Diagnostic and Statistical Manual of Mental Disorders, Fifth Edition (DSM-5) is a prominent tool for making diagnoses. Key features that differentiate situational depression from other mood disorders include the occurrence of depressed symptoms within three months of encountering a stressor and proof that the symptoms are a reaction to the stressor.

What kinds of changes or stresses in life can set off a case of situational depression?

Relationship issues, money problems, job loss, academic pressures, moving, illness, or loss of a loved one are just a few of the many life events and stresses that can set off situational depression. In vulnerable people, depressed symptoms can be triggered by anything that causes a substantial disturbance to their sense of stability, identity, or well-being.

Can other mental health issues coexist with situational depression?

It is also feasible for people to suffer from situational depression in addition to other mental health issues, like anxiety disorders, PTSD, or substance use disorders. It is essential for mental health practitioners to thoroughly evaluate and manage individuals with co-occurring illnesses, as they can make diagnosis more challenging. To effectively treat situational depression and co-occurring disorders, it is crucial to address underlying stresses and provide suitable therapies.

Can kids and teens be diagnosed with situational depression?

A diagnosis of situational depression can be made in children and adolescents when they undergo major life transitions or encounter intense stresses that cause them to exhibit depressed symptoms. However, developmental aspects, familial dynamics, and social stresses may all need to be carefully considered when diagnosing situational depression in this group. Irritability, social disengagement, academic decline, or physical symptoms are some of how children and adolescents with situational depression can present themselves, which may differ from how adults do it.

Can you tell me why it's crucial to rule out other mental or physiological issues when diagnosing situational depression?

To be sure the symptoms aren't just caused by something else, it's essential to rule out other medical or mental illnesses when diagnosing situational depression. A comprehensive medical evaluation is necessary to rule out physical ailments, including thyroid problems, vitamin shortages, or neurological issues, all of which can mirror depression symptoms. It may also be necessary to differentiate between mental disorders depending on the symptoms and progression of illness if they share specific characteristics, such as major depressive disorder, bipolar disorder, or adjustment disorder. A thorough evaluation conducted by a trained mental health expert is required to arrive at a correct diagnosis and formulate a suitable treatment strategy.

Does the diagnosis of situational depression rely on any particular evaluation instruments or standardized measures?

Mental health professionals may utilize standardized measures like the Beck Depression Inventory (BDI), the Patient Health Questionnaire-9 (PHQ-9), or the Hamilton Depression Rating Scale (HAM-D) to evaluate the severity of depressive symptoms and track treatment progress. However, there are no specific assessment tools for diagnosing situational depression. In conjunction with a comprehensive clinical interview and evaluation of stressors, these measures assist doctors in determining if a patient is suffering from situational depression by measuring the frequency and severity of depressed symptoms.

To make a diagnosis of situational depression, how significant are cultural factors?

It's important to take cultural norms, values, and ways of expressing pain into account when diagnosing situational depression because these factors might affect how symptoms manifest and whether or not a person seeks care. Mental health providers have a responsibility to their patients to be culturally competent and knowledgeable about the many ways in which patients' cultural backgrounds influence their stress levels, coping mechanisms, and perspectives on mental health treatment. A culturally responsive diagnostic and treatment plan can only be created after thoroughly understanding the patient's cultural background and environment.

Will treatment be necessary for situational depression to go away?

If the source of stress or triggering event is dealt with, adjusted to, or eliminated, the depressive symptoms associated with situational depression may go away without treatment. However, everyone's symptoms are different in length and intensity, and some people need help from experts to manage their symptoms and get better. Despite the common belief that situational depression is just a passing phase, the reality is that if left untreated, symptoms can linger or even worsen, causing significant impairment in functioning and a decline in overall quality of life.

If situational depression is left untreated, what may happen?

Prolonged emotional suffering, poor social and occupational functioning, strained interpersonal connections, and an increased chance of developing chronic or recurring depressive episodes are some of the adverse outcomes that can result from untreated situational depression. In addition to affecting mental health, physical health, and immunological function, persistent depressed symptoms can worsen or cause other mental health issues to develop or worsen. It is crucial to intervene early and get proper therapy for situational depression because it can exacerbate the risk of self-harm, suicidal thoughts, and suicide attempts if left untreated.

During a diagnosis of situational depression, how may loved ones and carers best assist the patient?

One way that loved ones can help someone going through a diagnosis of situational depression is by listening to their stories and offering words of encouragement and validation. They can help you recognise what's causing your depression, connect you with options for mental health or professional support, and motivate you to take care of yourself and learn new coping mechanisms. Keeping lines of communication open, showing empathy, and creating a supportive and non-judgmental atmosphere can make people feel understood and appreciated during this challenging period.

What are some typical difficulties that people have when trying to get a diagnosis of situational depression?

People may be reluctant to seek a diagnosis for situational depression due to several factors, such as financial limitations, a lack of knowledge about available resources or treatment options, cultural beliefs or misconceptions about depression, a lack of trust in mental health professionals, a lack of transportation options, and the stigma associated with mental health issues. Furthermore, people may downplay or blame their symptoms entirely on outside influences, refusing to seek medical attention until their symptoms worsen to an incapacitating level.

When diagnosing situational depression, how can doctors tell it apart from other mood disorders?

To distinguish situational depression from other mood disorders, healthcare experts closely examine the timing of depressed symptoms in connection to specific stresses or life events. Depressive symptoms usually disappear after the stressor is dealt with or adjusted to, and situational depression is defined by its appearance within three months after experiencing the stressor. Depressive symptoms in other mood disorders, such as bipolar disorder or major depressive disorder, on the other hand, can be more persistent, recurrent, or unrelated to particular causes. Differentiating situational depression from other mood disorders also involves looking at the degree, length, and functional impairment linked to depressive symptoms.

While designing a course of treatment for people with situational depression, what factors are most important to keep in mind?

When designing a program to help people who are suffering from situational depression, it's essential to take several factors into account. These include figuring out what's causing their depression, teaching them coping mechanisms and how to deal with stress, using evidence-based treatments like psychotherapy or medication (such as antidepressants) when needed, building social support systems, encouraging healthy habits like getting enough sleep, eating well, and exercising are Optimising outcomes and supporting recovery requires a treatment approach that is tailored to the individual's needs, preferences, and cultural setting.

To what extent may psychotherapy alleviate situational depression?

In the treatment of situational depression, psychotherapy (also known as talk therapy) can offer several benefits. These include creating a safe and accepting environment to talk about feelings, learning to recognise when we're thinking negatively, building resilience and self-awareness, improving our ability to communicate and connect with others, and ultimately, helping us feel more in control of our lives and how we deal with stressful situations. Common psychotherapy treatments for treating situational depression include cognitive-behavioral therapy (CBT), interpersonal therapy (IPT), and supportive therapy, all of which can be adapted to meet the unique requirements and objectives of each patient.

When dealing with situational depression, what part does medicine play?

When symptoms of situational depression are severe, long-lasting, or severely limiting daily functioning, medication may be considered as a component of the treatment approach. Medications that block the reuptake of serotonin and norepinephrine, known as antidepressants, can help ease symptoms of depression and speed up the healing process. The drug is an essential part of treating situational depression, but it isn't a panacea. A healthcare provider should closely monitor drug use, taking into account side effects, contraindications, and individual circumstances. When deciding on a course of therapy, the patient and healthcare provider must work together, considering the patient's symptoms, preferences, and any concerns about side effects.

Chapter Four

Treatments for situational depression (an adjustment condition characterized by sad mood)

What kinds of treatments are there for depression that occurs in specific situations?

Psychotherapy, medication, or a mix of the two are the usual treatment choices for situational depression. Treatment for depression may involve medication, such as antidepressants, and psychotherapy, such as CBT, IPT, or supportive therapy, to address dysfunctional ways of thinking, behaving, and coping.

Does situational depression respond well to psychotherapy?

If you are suffering from situational depression, psychotherapy can help. It helps people deal with difficult situations by teaching them coping mechanisms, providing emotional support, and outlining strategies. For instance, research has demonstrated that cognitive-behavioral therapy (CBT) helps people recognise and change unhelpful ways of thinking and establish more positive routines for dealing with stressful situations.

In most cases, how long does it take to get better from situational depression?

The length of time someone needs to be treated for situational depression depends on several factors, including how well they respond to treatment, how bad their symptoms are, and what stresses them out in the first place. Ongoing treatment and support may be required to manage symptoms effectively in some cases of situational depression, while in others, it may fade if the stressor is treated or acclimated.

Does situational depression often need the use of antidepressants?

In cases where symptoms of situational depression are severe, long-lasting, or severely limiting in their ability to carry out everyday tasks, a doctor may recommend antidepressants. Medication is not usually required for those with situational depression, but it is frequently used in conjunction with psychotherapy.

Could you please tell me the possible adverse effects of antidepressants?

The following are some of the most common adverse effects of antidepressants: nausea, vertigo, lethargy, dry mouth, increased appetite, and erectile dysfunction. It is critical to keep track of any changes or adverse reactions while taking medicine and talk to your doctor about possible side effects.

Are there any ways to handle situational sadness through lifestyle adjustments?

Making adjustments to one's way of life can be pretty helpful in dealing with situational depression. Thus, the answer is yes. Improving mood and general well-being can be achieved by regular exercise, a nutritious diet, sufficient sleep, relaxation techniques (such as mindfulness or deep breathing), and reaching out to social support.

Is treatment necessary for a full recovery from situational depression?

If the stressor or trigger is short-lived and can be adequately handled or adjusted to, situational depression may go away without treatment altogether. You can speed up your recovery and lessen the likelihood of your symptoms worsening or staying the same by getting professional help and using coping mechanisms.

What can I do if I think I may be suffering from situational depression or if I know someone who may be?

It is critical to advocate seeking help from a mental health expert if you or someone you know is believed to be suffering from situational depression. Individuals can benefit from an evaluation, diagnosis, and treatment plan a licensed therapist or counsellor explicitly developed. Helping someone who is suffering from situational depression benefits from your empathy, understanding, and practical help.

When it comes to controlling situational depression, are there any complementary or alternative therapies that can be useful?

When it comes to dealing with situational depression, some people may find relief through alternative or complementary therapies. Stress reduction, relaxation, and general health may all be possible outcomes of yoga, acupuncture, mindfulness meditation, or massage therapy. It's important to talk to a healthcare professional to ensure these choices are supplemented rather than substitute treatments supported by evidence.

To help maintain my mental health when I'm going through a tough patch, what kinds of self-care practices can I include in my regular schedule?

Taking care of oneself can be helpful when dealing with situational depression. To take care of oneself, make sure to get enough sleep, work out regularly, practice relaxation techniques like deep breathing or progressive muscle relaxation, eat a diet full of fruits, vegetables, and whole grains, set boundaries to avoid overspending, surround yourself with supportive people, and do things that make you happy.

While receiving treatment for situational depression, how can I keep tabs on how I'm doing and whether my symptoms are getting better?

It can be good to keep a mood journal or use a mood-tracking app to keep tabs on how your symptoms are changing and how far along you are in the recovery process from situational depression. Keep track of your thoughts, behaviours, daily mood ratings, and any significant events or stressors. During therapy sessions or appointments, please share this information with your healthcare practitioner so they may look for trends, gauge how healthy treatment is working, and make any necessary adjustments to your treatment plan.

If my symptoms of situational depression return or intensify while I am receiving treatment, what am I to do?

It is crucial to contact your healthcare practitioner without delay if you encounter a recurrence or worsening of symptoms while receiving therapy for situational depression. By working together, you can reevaluate your treatment plan, identify and address any stresses or triggers that may have contributed to the relapse, and improve the efficacy of intervention. Effective symptom management and prevention of further deterioration require prioritizing self-care, seeking help from loved ones, and sticking to the treatment plan.

What can I do to be there for a family member or friend while they get treatment for situational depression?

When a loved one is getting therapy for situational depression, it's essential to be there for them emotionally and provide them with practical help. Motivate them to participate in self-care activities, attend therapy sessions regularly, and take their medicine as directed. Reassure and encourage while attentively listening without passing judgment. You can offer to go with them to appointments or pitch in with chores around the house if they need it. To empathize with their struggles and provide practical assistance, familiarise yourself with depression and the services that are accessible.

If you or someone you know is suffering from situational depression, what options are available to help?

People who are looking for information and support regarding situational depression can get it through a variety of online resources, such as mental health websites, hotlines, support groups, and forums. Regional and national mental health organisations may offer referral services, educational materials, and resources. Individuals suffering from situational depression may also benefit from self-help resources such as books, podcasts, and apps that address depression management and coping skills.

How can I talk to my boss or principal about my situational melancholy and ask for help if needed?

When discussing situational depression with your employer or school, it's crucial to put your own needs first and prioritize your well-being. To confidently discuss your situation, arrange a meeting with a supervisor, human resources representative, or school counsellor. Make it crystal clear how your depression hinders your capacity to carry out duties and take part in activities, and suggest concrete adjustments that might help your mental health, including more leeway in scheduling, less work, or more time to complete tasks. If requested, please include medical records from your provider and restate your intention to carry out your duties with the help you need.

Could I experience a recurrence of situational depression if I were to face comparable stresses or triggers in the future?

Recurrence of situational depression is likely in the future when comparable stresses or triggers are experienced. People with a history of situational depression may be more prone to experiencing depressive symptoms if they encounter significant life changes, difficulties, or losses. However, one can lessen the likelihood of a recurrence and increase resilience by actively managing stress, sticking to healthy routines, getting appropriate support, and applying coping mechanisms learned from earlier episodes.

As a grieving person, how can I tell the difference between the normal range of emotions and the signs of situational depression?

It might be difficult to tell the difference between the symptoms of situational depression and more common emotions like sadness or loss. Feelings of melancholy or distress can come and go in response to life's experiences. Still, situational depression is characterized by symptoms that are more severe, long-lasting, and disruptive to everyday living. Please track how long your symptoms last, how bad they are, and how they affect your relationships, self-care, and employment. Professional evaluation should be sought if symptoms last for a long time or significantly impair coping abilities; this could be a sign of situational depression.

Is there a way for those with situational depression to connect with others who are going through the same thing?

People who suffer from situational depression can find help through peer support programs or community-based initiatives. Depression and coping mechanisms may be the subject of support groups, seminars, or instructional activities hosted by local religious institutions, community centres, or mental health agencies. People dealing with situational depression can also find support, validation, and encouragement through online platforms and social media groups that are specifically devoted to mental health advocacy and peer support. Volunteering or participating in leisure activities can also help people meet new people, increasing their feeling of belonging and purpose.

What are some ways to deal with stress and become more resilient so that you can avoid or lessen the severity of situational depression?

To manage stress and build resilience, engage in self-care practices like exercise, mindfulness meditation, and relaxation techniques. Prioritize your well-being by establishing healthy boundaries. Nurture social connections and seek support from friends, family, or support groups. Find purpose and meaning in hobbies, interests, or volunteer work. Set realistic goals and focus on solutions rather than problems when feeling down. Please seek professional help or therapy when you need it to develop coping skills and emotional resilience.

Every day, how can I deal with the signs of situational depression?

Staying consistent, doing things you enjoy, exercising regularly, learning relaxation techniques, and getting enough sleep are all self-care habits that can help with situational depression. It's also important to talk to people who will be there for you and get professional help if you need it.

For those who suffer from situational depression, what are some excellent ways to deal with the stresses in their lives?

It's helpful to use problem-solving techniques like breaking tasks into smaller ones, reaching out to trusted friends and family for support, getting some exercise to burn off steam, practising mindfulness or meditation to calm down, and getting enough sleep to manage stress.

What steps can I take to strengthen my ability to bounce back from setbacks caused by situational depression?

To build resilience, one must learn to cope with adversity, cultivate positive relationships, keep a positive outlook, establish attainable objectives, reflect on and learn from one's experiences, and, when necessary, seek help from mental health experts or support groups.

When dealing with situational depression, how important is social support?

When dealing with situational depression, it is essential to have social support since it can offer emotional affirmation, practical help, and a feeling of belonging. It is helpful to cultivate supportive relationships and seek advice and encouragement from trusted others to improve one's well-being and reduce feelings of loneliness.

Does anyone know of any services or support groups that are tailored to those who suffer from situational depression?

People who suffer from situational depression do have access to resources and support groups. Support groups and educational courses on coping mechanisms, stress management, and emotional wellness may be available through community centres, internet forums, and local mental health organizations. Individualized assistance and direction can also be obtained through consulting with mental health experts or engaging in therapy.

My loved one is suffering from situational depression; how can I help them?

To be there for a loved one going through situational depression is to listen with empathy, validate and encourage them, help them with everyday activities if they need it, and encourage them to get professional help when they need it. Focus on providing understanding and support rather than passing judgment or making criticisms.

To alleviate the signs of situational depression, what kinds of self-care activities may one do?

It is important to prioritize self-care practices such as getting enough sleep, eating a balanced diet, exercising regularly, practising relaxation techniques like progressive muscle relaxation or deep breathing, spending time in nature, and doing things that make you happy or relaxed.

How can I keep my situational depression from getting worse when things get tough?

It's essential to take steps to manage stress, find people you can lean on for support, take care of yourself, set appropriate boundaries, and get professional help if your symptoms get out of hand to keep situational depression from getting worse. A person must prioritise self-awareness and act proactively when new symptoms or triggers arise.

How can one deal with the destructive emotions and thoughts that come with situational depression?

When dealing with situational depression, it's essential to work on challenging negative self-talk, replacing illogical thoughts with more reasonable and positive ones through cognitive restructuring techniques, and doing things that make you feel good about yourself.

Relax techniques and mindfulness meditation can foster a nonjudgmental awareness of one's thoughts and emotions.

To take care of my mental health while coping with situational depression, how can I set reasonable limits in my relationships?

Being a good relationship partner means being honest and direct about what you need, being firm about your limits, and prioritising time for yourself and your health. It's critical to be self-aware, know when to say "no," and surround yourself with encouraging people who also value and honour your boundaries.

In a professional or academic context, what are some ways to deal with situational depression?

The following are some strategies for managing situational depression in the workplace or academic setting: talking to your boss or professor about it and asking for help if you need it; making a list of everything you need to do and sticking to it; taking frequent breaks to recharge; reaching out to people you work or school with for support; and using resources like campus counselling services or employee assistance programs.

While coping with situational depression, how can I keep myself motivated and focused on my objectives?

When you set tiny, attainable goals, break them into manageable chunks, celebrate achievement, and practice self-compassion when failures occur, you maintain your motivation. Overcoming self-doubt helps you reflect on what you're good at, reach out to people for encouragement, and do things that matter.

When dealing with situational depression, what am I to do if I have a setback or relapse?

When you encounter difficulties or a setback, it's crucial to take care of yourself, seek help from loved ones or mental health experts, and review your methods of coping and treatment regimen. Locate the stresses or triggers causing the relapse and figure out how to deal with them. Always be kind and gentle with yourself when you have difficulties; this is a natural component of the healing process.

How can I deal with situational sadness by making mindfulness and relaxation a regular part of my life?

One way to deal with situational depression is to practice mindfulness or relaxation techniques regularly. These can help you feel more at ease and less stressed out. Every day, take a few minutes to focus on your breathing, PMR (progressive muscular relaxation), or guided visualization. If you want to learn to be more present and mindful in your daily life, you might want to look into yoga or mindfulness meditation.

In the treatment of situational depression, what part does exercise play?

Physical exercise has several positive effects on mood, general health, and the management of situational depression, including alleviating depressive symptoms and increasing energy levels. On most days of the week, try to get in 30 minutes of moderate-intensity activity, like a brisk walk, swim, or bike ride. Look for things to do that suit your interests, skills, and talents and that you can actually do.

How can I deal with situational depression in a way that promotes regular self-care?

Making time for self-care a regular part of your routine and making your health a priority are two ways to manage situational depression effectively. Make time for things that bring you joy and help you recharge—like reading, going for walks, engaging in a hobby, or taking a relaxing bath—as part of your self-care routine. Make self-care a regular priority by setting reminders or blocking off time in your calendar.

What are some tried-and-true methods for dealing with situational depression-related sleep disruptions?

A regular sleep pattern, a soothing bedtime ritual, a reduction in coffee and screen time in the hours leading up to bed, and a conducive sleep environment are all helpful in managing sleep disruptions caused by situational depression. Try relaxation techniques like deep breathing or progressive muscle relaxation to get ready for sleep. For additional help, talk to a doctor if your sleep problems don't go away.

When dealing with situational depression, how can I combat the emotions of being alone or isolated?

Contacting encouraging loved ones or joining a support group are great ways to combat feeling alone or isolated. Maintaining social connections and fighting feelings of isolation can be achieved through scheduling regular, albeit tiny, social events or outings. To meet new people and broaden your social circle, you might want to think about volunteering or joining an exciting organization.

How can one deal with stressful situations healthily, especially if they are suffering from situational depression?

To manage stress that can worsen symptoms of situational depression, try deep breathing exercises or mindfulness meditation. Exercising can help you relax and release endorphins. Reach out to loved ones for social support. And remember to set boundaries to protect your time and energy. You might also consider getting therapy or professional assistance to build resilience and efficient coping mechanisms.

While dealing with situational depression, how can I maintain an optimistic outlook?

The good things in your life and the attainable goals you set for yourself for the future are the building blocks of hope and optimism that you may cultivate. Make a habit of being thankful by naming and savouring all the blessings in your life. To feel lifted and inspired, surround yourself with positive, encouraging people. Take part in what makes you happy and fulfilled, and remember that tough times are fleeting, and you can get through anything.

Supporting a loved one with situational depression

My loved one is suffering from situational depression; how can I help them?

The best way to help a loved one who is suffering from situational depression is to listen to them without passing judgment and to validate how they are feeling. In addition to providing practical assistance with day-to-day obligations, you should encourage them to seek professional treatment if needed.

Do you know how to talk to a family member or friend who is suffering from situational depression?

Paying close attention, acknowledging their emotions, and showing empathy are all parts of effective communication. Do not belittle their experiences or provide unwanted advice. Be present to lend an ear and tell them they have your support instead.

My loved one is suffering from situational depression; how can I encourage them to get treatment?

Suggest that your loved one see a doctor or mental health expert about their symptoms and offer to help them locate one. You can offer to go with them to their support appointments if they feel comfortable.

What can I do if the person I'm trying to help with situational depression refuses or downplays the severity of their symptoms?

No matter how much you care about a loved one, you must always tell them how much you appreciate their independence. Never compel or force someone to seek help; instead, keep offering support and urging them to do so. Reassure them that you are available to listen and provide assistance anytime they need it.

While coping with situational depression, how can I assist a loved one in continuing with their regular activities and obligations?

Provide them with practical assistance by taking on some of their obligations or tasks if they feel overwhelmed. They should stick to a schedule that allows them to eat healthily, get adequate sleep, and do things they like.

What are the warning signals that someone I care about is experiencing a worsening of their situational depression, and what can I do to assist?

Symptoms of situational depression that could be getting worse include feeling less motivated to engage in once enjoyable activities, having trouble sleeping or eating, and proclaiming feelings of worthlessness or hopelessness. If you observe any of these indicators, you must support your loved one and gently urge them to get professional help.

How can I be there for a loved one who is suffering from situational depression emotionally without letting myself become overwhelmed?

As a carer for a loved one dealing with situational depression, you must put your own needs first. Protect your emotional and mental well-being by establishing limits and seeking help when needed. Remember that taking care of yourself and breaks are perfectly acceptable.

Carers of people with situational depression may benefit from knowing about various support groups and resources. How true is it?

Carers of people with situational depression can get assistance through local mental health organizations or internet forums. Joining one of these communities can help you connect with others who are going through the same things and can give you advice and support. You can think about going to a counsellor or therapist one-on-one for further assistance.

How can I help a family member or friend who is suffering from situational depression to take part in self-care routines?

Bring up the subject of self-care calmly and nonjudgmentally, stressing how important it is for one's mental health to take care of oneself. Go for a stroll, practice relaxation techniques, or try out a new pastime as a couple to take care of yourself. They need your patience and encouragement while they figure out how to take care of themselves.

How can I assist a loved one who is suffering from situational depression in overcoming the difficulties that bring on their symptoms?

Please work with the person you care about to determine what stresses them out and how to deal with them. Prompt them to exercise, learn calming techniques, or consult a doctor if they need it. As they face challenging circumstances, extend your support and empathy.

How can I create a safe space where my loved one suffering from situational depression can feel supported and understood?

Encourage your loved one to open up to you by listening to them without passing judgment on their feelings or what they have been through. Instead of reacting negatively or criticizing, try offering validation and reassurance. Make it a place where people can freely express themselves and get help.

When a loved one suffering from situational depression refuses to accept assistance, what can I do?

Be sensitive to your loved one's wishes while subtly urging them to weigh the pros and disadvantages of reaching out for assistance. Show your support and empathy without making demands or passing judgment. Reassure them that you are available to listen and provide assistance anytime they need it.

How can I help my loved one who is suffering from situational depression by learning more about it?

Seek out credible resources, including mental health organizations, books, or internet resources, to educate yourself on situational depression. Consider consulting with mental health experts for advice and information and attending educational seminars or workshops.

When a loved one is dealing with situational depression, how can I demonstrate compassion and understanding?

Listen attentively and without passing judgment on what your loved one is saying as a way to demonstrate empathy. Reassure them that they are not alone and validate their emotions. Being present and sympathetic is more critical than downplaying their experiences or giving unsolicited advice.

My loved one is suffering from situational depression; what can I do to assist them in creating reasonable expectations and objectives for their recovery?

Get your loved one to make modest, attainable goals that align with what they can do and what they have available to them. As they strive to achieve their objectives, be there to offer your support and encouragement and to rejoice in their victories. They need to know that getting better is a process and that obstacles are expected.

How can I encourage a family member or friend who is suffering from situational depression to lead a healthy lifestyle?

Stress the importance of getting enough sleep, eating a balanced diet, and exercising regularly to your loved one. Help each other out by offering to work out together, make healthy meals, or have a regular schedule for when you both go to bed. Set a good example by engaging in healthy behaviours yourself.

My loved one is struggling with situational depression; how can I assist them in developing resilience and coping mechanisms?

Suggest that your loved one focus on resilience by meditating or mindfulness, surrounding themselves with positive people, and learning to solve problems effectively. As kids try new things and adjust to new situations, be there to offer your support and encouragement.

What can I do to assist a family member or friend who is suffering from situational depression in navigating relationships and social situations?

The best way to help a loved one deal with relationships and social interactions is to be there for them and offer advice and encouragement. Offer to go with them to social occasions if they're feeling nervous or overwhelmed, and encourage them to talk honestly about their needs and boundaries with others. When dealing with challenging interactions, be a sympathetic listener and offer reassurance.

Despite my best efforts to offer assistance, my loved one's situational depression continues to worsen. What can I do to help?

If your loved one's situational depression persists or worsens despite your best efforts, it is recommended that they consult a therapist or counsellor for further assistance. Be there for them and help them discover what they need: resources or treatment. Reassure them that reaching out for assistance is healthy and that getting expert help is a significant first step on the road to recovery.

While helping a loved one who is suffering from situational depression, how can I ensure my mental health is not negatively impacted?

Setting boundaries, reaching out to loved ones for support, and engaging in stress-management practices like mindfulness or relaxation exercises should all be your priorities regarding self-care. Get some rest when needed, and do things that make you happy. Think about getting help processing your feelings and experiences through therapy or counselling. You can better assist your loved one if you care for yourself first.

How does adolescent and kid situational depression show itself?

Physical symptoms such as headaches or stomachaches, as well as irritation, melancholy, changes in eating or sleep habits, social disengagement, and academic decline, are all possible manifestations of situational depression in children and adolescents. Keep an eye out for any changes in behaviour or mood and get expert assistance if necessary.

What specific difficulties do elderly persons with situational depression encounter?

Challenges that older persons may encounter when suffering from situational depression include intensified feelings of loneliness or isolation, long-term health issues, diminished autonomy, and grief from loved ones' deaths. To overcome these obstacles, offering social support, encouraging participation in purposeful activities, and guaranteeing access to suitable mental health treatment is essential.

When people from different cultural backgrounds experience situational sadness, how does it impact them?

Different cultural beliefs, values, and coping techniques might cause situational sadness to present differently in people from various cultural backgrounds. When providing support to persons from varied backgrounds who are experiencing situational depression, it is crucial to take cultural aspects into account. These considerations include the stigma around mental health, family relationships, and the availability of culturally appropriate care.

Do people in demanding or high-stress occupations experience any particular kinds of stress?

People who work in notoriously stressful occupations may have to deal with extra challenges like long hours, tight deadlines, difficult coworkers, or even horrific experiences. These stresses can exacerbate situational depression. People in these fields need our support, work-life balance encouragement, and mental health resources.

What is the effect of traumatic experiences or other unfavourable life circumstances on people who suffer from situational depression?

Situational depression can be brought on or worsened by traumatic experiences or adverse life circumstances like grief, mistreatment, catastrophic occurrences, or economic hardships. People who have been through traumatic experiences often deal with not only depression but also symptoms like flashbacks, hypervigilance, or avoidance behaviours. Providing trauma-informed care and addressing symptoms associated with trauma is of the utmost importance.

When helping members of the LGBTQ+ community who are experiencing situational depression, what factors are specific to this population?

Situational depression can be exacerbated by the unique stresses that LGBTQ+ individuals may encounter, including but not limited to rejection, stigma, discrimination, and issues relating to their identity. It is critical to address the unique problems connected to gender identity and sexual orientation, provide LGBTQ+-affirming mental health care, and foster an accepting and safe space for all people.

To what extent does situational depression impact people who live with long-term health issues or physical impairments?

It's worth noting that situational depression can worsen physical symptoms and affect the quality of life for those with impairments or chronic health issues. It's critical to give these people holistic treatment that takes their mental and physical health into account, as well as support that is specific to their requirements.

When people from marginalized or minority groups experience situational depression, what socioeconomic and cultural elements play a role?

Cultural and societal variables, including prejudice, systematic oppression, socioeconomic inequality, and inadequate healthcare access, can exacerbate situational depression in minority or oppressed communities. To overcome these systemic obstacles, culturally competent care that recognizes and values people's identities and experiences must be provided.

What is the impact of situational depression on carers of loved ones with long-term health conditions or disabilities?

As a result of the mental and emotional toll that caring for a loved one with a chronic disease or disability can take, carers may suffer from situational depression. Overwhelm, depression, or burnout could set in if they put the needs of those they care about ahead of their own. Providing carers with support, respite care, and mental health services is paramount.

When dealing with situational depression, what are the specific obstacles that people living in rural or outlying areas encounter?

People living in more isolated or rural locations may encounter difficulties like isolation, stigma, extensive travel times to healthcare facilities, and a lack of mental health treatments. It might be much more challenging to get help when these circumstances are present, which can worsen situational depression. People living in remote locations must have access to community-based support services, expand telehealth options, and eliminate obstacles to care.

How can situational depression impact those going through significant life changes like retirement, divorce, or moving?

The loss of one's identity, one's routine, and one's social relationships, all of which are connected with significant life upheavals, can lead to situational depression. During these changes, people may experience emotions of loss, loneliness, and uncertainty.

As people face and adapt to these changes, offering them resources, affirmation, and support is critical.

When helping members of the military or veterans cope with situational depression, what factors are specific to their needs?

Specific unique stresses experienced by military personnel and veterans, such as exposure to conflict, trauma associated with deployment, or difficulties with reintegration, can lead to situational depression. Furthermore, service members may be reluctant to seek care due to the stigma associated with mental health issues. Promoting access to mental health treatments, treating military-specific stresses, and providing culturally competent and trauma-informed care are all critical.

When people are facing severe financial problems or have lost their jobs, how does situational depression affect them?

The stress, uncertainty, and lack of stability brought on by financial troubles or losing a job might contribute to situational depression. A person's economic status might contribute to feelings of inadequacy, despair, and shame. It is essential to offer support, resources, and aid with basic requirements to help people deal with these stresses and feel more in control of their lives.

In times of crisis, what are the specific things to keep in mind when helping those who are suffering from situational depression?

The stress, grief, and loss that accompany emergencies and natural disasters can make a person feel trapped in a depressive episode. After such occurrences, people could feel anxious, depressed, or suffer from post-traumatic stress disorder. Helping people deal with the emotional fallout of emergencies and natural disasters requires quick crisis care, access to mental health treatments, and community-based resources.

What is the impact of situational depression on those moving to a new nation, such as immigrants or refugees?

While adjusting to a new nation, culture, and language, immigrants or refugees may face the difficulties of situational depression. They might experience trauma as a result of forced relocation, social isolation, prejudice, or problems adjusting to their new environment. Immigrants and refugees may face specific stresses during relocation; it is crucial to offer culturally relevant support, resources, and access to mental health care.

How can we best assist those who are homeless or otherwise suffering housing instability due to situational depression? What are the specific factors to consider in this case?

People who are homeless or have unstable housing are more likely to suffer from situational depression because of the stress, trauma, and instability that come with their living circumstances. Mental health treatment and other support services may be complex for them to access as well. People who are homeless or have unstable housing must have access to outreach, housing aid, and wraparound services that deal with their immediate needs as well as their mental health issues.

For those who have survived abuse or violence at the hands of another, what are the effects of situational depression?

The trauma, anxiety, and psychological suffering felt by survivors of interpersonal abuse or violence can lead to situational depression. Along with depression symptoms, they may also experience symptoms like hypervigilance, low self-esteem, or flashbacks. Survivors of interpersonal violence or abuse must have access to trauma-informed care, safety planning, and supporting resources to heal and rehabilitate.

When dealing with the criminal justice system, what specific difficulties do people with situational depression encounter?

People who are in prison or have dealt with the criminal justice system may encounter particular difficulties, including prejudice, seclusion, inadequate mental health treatment, and trauma resulting from their encounters with the system. The stresses and lack of resources that come with being incarcerated can make situational depression worse. It is crucial to offer screenings, treatments, and support services to help inmates with their mental health issues and encourage their recovery.

What effects can situational depression have on people coping with addiction or substance use disorders?

The physiological, social, and psychological impacts of substance use can lead to situational depression in those who are coping with substance use disorders or addiction. A vicious cycle of drug misuse and mental health issues can develop when depression and substance use disorders occur together. Supporting recovery and well-being for individuals with co-occurring disorders requires therapy that integrates substance use and mental health concerns.

How can we best assist those residing in nursing homes or other long-term care institutions who are dealing with situational depression?

Situational depression can be a real issue for people residing in nursing homes or other long-term care facilities. It is because these individuals may be dealing with issues like social isolation, a decline in their health, or a loss of independence. They might also have trouble getting the help they need for their mental health or taking part in things that matter to them. Enhancing residents' quality of life and emotional well-being within long-term care facilities can be achieved by promoting person-centred care, social engagement, and mental health assistance.

Chapter Five

Co-occurring disorders and difficulties with situational depression

In most cases, what other mental health issues often coexist with situational depression?

Anxiety disorders, PTSD, substance use disorders, adjustment disorders involving anxiety, and situational depression frequently occur together. These co-occurring disorders can make situational depression more challenging to diagnose and treat, necessitating an all-encompassing strategy.

In what ways can situational depression raise the likelihood of acquiring MDD or chronic depression?

Prolonged or severe instances of situational depression can heighten the likelihood of developing chronic depression or MDD, even though it usually subsides once the stressor is no longer present or coping mechanisms are implemented. In the absence of adequate coping mechanisms and social support, situational depression has the potential to progress into a more severe and long-lasting form of depression.

Are there any specific physical health issues that often go hand in hand with situational depression?

Conditions include impaired immunological function, heart disease, gastrointestinal issues, chronic pain, and other physical health problems that are more likely to develop or worsen in people with situational depression. Inflammation and hormone imbalances are two potential side effects of the stress response that can accompany depression and have a detrimental impact on general health.

How does situational depression impact executive functioning and cognitive function?

Problems with focus, memory, decision-making, and problem-solving may manifest as impaired cognitive function and executive functioning due to situational depression. Cognitive distortions, often known as negative thought patterns, can make it hard to function daily and make people feel even worse about themselves.

Is there a correlation between situational depression and interpersonal and social difficulties?

Relationship problems, social withdrawal or isolation, and poor academic or work performance are all symptoms of situational depression. People may find it challenging to keep in touch with friends and family, complete tasks, or enjoy free time. Loneliness, estrangement, or rejection might occur when these interpersonal difficulties arise.

How can situational depression impact the quality and consistency of sleep?

Illnesses related to sleep, such as insomnia or hypersomnia, can be brought on by situational depression. People may struggle to sleep, remain asleep, or get restorative sleep. Depressive symptoms, including anger, reduced functioning, and daytime exhaustion, can be worsened by poor sleep quality.

What are the things that put people with situational depression at risk of hurting themselves or thinking about suicide?

In circumstances where individuals experience feelings of being overwhelmed by stressors or do not have suitable coping mechanisms, situational depression might heighten the risk of self-harm or suicidal thoughts. Hopelessness, social isolation, substance abuse, traumatic experiences, and the availability of self-harming tools are all potential risk factors for self-harm and suicidal thoughts.

What effects does situational depression have on one's ability to function and quality of life generally?

Situational depression can have a significant impact on many aspects of a person's life, including their ability to function in the workplace or school, their relationships, their leisure time, and their physical health. Reduced productivity, poor life pleasure, and trouble carrying out one's duties and obligations are all possible outcomes.

Is there a correlation between situational depression and monetary or social issues?

A person's ability to earn a living, the cost of medical treatment, and the ease with which they can handle their money can all be negatively impacted by situational depression. Poor cognitive function and decreased work productivity can lead to these problems. Socioeconomic differences might hinder access to mental health care and support services.

If you are a parent or carer, how does situational depression affect your role?

Situational depression can impact a person's capacity to care for others, including their ability to offer emotional support, stick to routines, or meet the needs of others who rely on them. It can be challenging for parents or carers dealing with situational depression to provide adequate care for others because of feelings of shame, inadequacy, or overwhelm.

To what extent can situational depression impact a person's ability to succeed in school or at work?

Students and workers affected by situational depression may find it challenging to focus and finish assignments, which in turn affects their academic or vocational performance. People may struggle to complete tasks on time, operate at their typical level, or concentrate on schoolwork or jobs. Success in school and the workplace may suffer due to these difficulties in the future.

What effects can situational depression have on the ability to make decisions and take risks?

The ability to make sound decisions and the frequency with which one engages in potentially harmful actions are both negatively impacted by situational sadness. People may struggle to think through potential outcomes, make good decisions, or put long-term objectives ahead of short-term rewards. Involvement in activities that worsen depressed symptoms, impulsivity, and irresponsibility are possible outcomes.

When it comes to physical self-care and health behaviours, how does situational depression factor in?

People suffering from situational depression may find it difficult to prioritize their physical well-being, which can result in a lack of attention to essential needs like healthy eating, regular exercise, good hygiene, and medical treatment. Appetite changes, weight fluctuations, and sleep disturbances are all possible side effects. When people don't take care of themselves, their depression symptoms and general health can worsen.

To what extent does situational depression impair the capacity to establish and maintain relationships with social support systems?

The ability or desire to seek assistance from others can be impacted by situational depression, which in turn can impact social support networks. Some people with mental health issues may isolate themselves, avoid reaching out to others for help, or feel stigmatized for seeking help. Isolation and loneliness, although there, can become much more severe as a result, making it harder to cope and recuperate.

What happens when situational depression goes undiagnosed or gets inadequate treatment?

With time, symptoms of untreated or inadequately managed situational depression can become chronic, return, or even worsen. A person may become more prone to various mental health issues, have trouble functioning for an extended period, or adopt unhealthy ways of coping. Early and effective treatment of situational depression can enhance outcomes and reduce the risk of long-term consequences.

To what extent does situational depression influence interpersonal dynamics within families?

Tension, disagreement, or breaks in communication can be caused by situational depression, which can strain family dynamics and relationships. Family members of a depressed person may find it difficult to empathize with or provide emotional support, which can lead to resentment and miscommunication. Family therapy or support programmes could help overcome these relational obstacles.

The question is, how can situational depression affect treatment adherence and participation?

By affecting motivation, self-efficacy, and perceived benefit of therapies, situational depression can affect treatment adherence and engagement. People may find it challenging to implement treatment plans, keep their therapy appointments, or take their medications as prescribed. It is important to address barriers to treatment adherence and offer individualized assistance.

What role do cultural and social elements play in the development of situational depression?

Cultural and sociocultural factors can interact with situational depression, impacting how people see, talk about, and manage their depression. Attitudes towards mental health, help-seeking behaviours, and the stigma around depression can be influenced by cultural ideas, values, and conventions. When offering assistance and treatments for situational depression, it is crucial to take cultural background and identity into account.

When it comes to coping mechanisms and resilience, what does situational depression imply?

Situational depression can test one's resilience and ability to cope, especially for those without social support systems or adaptive coping mechanisms. People can develop resilience and better handle adversity with the help of psychoeducation, stress management strategies, and interventions that increase social support.

When dealing with existential issues, meaning-making, and spirituality, how does situational depression manifest?

People suffering from situational depression may find solace and direction in contemplating spiritual or existential views, searching for meaning and purpose in their lives, and wrestling with existential problems. Addressing these existential issues and building resilience in the face of situational depression may be supported by spiritual activities, existential therapy, or religious communities.

After suffering from situational depression, how much time does it usually take to feel better?

Many factors, which include the intensity of the stressor, the presence or absence of social support, the development of coping mechanisms, and the degree to which treatment is adhered to, contribute to the fact that the rate of recovery from situational depression varies considerably among individuals. Once the source of stress is eliminated or coping strategies are put into place, many people with situational depression report a resolution of their symptoms within a few months. It may take longer for certain people, or they may need constant support to become well.

To overcome situational depression, what are the most important factors?

Resolving the root cause of the stress, learning effective coping mechanisms, strengthening resilience, and regaining general health are all necessary steps towards overcoming situational depression. It requires therapy or counselling to work through feelings and develop healthy coping mechanisms, social support from loved ones, self-care activities like exercise and mindfulness, and, in extreme circumstances, medication to alleviate symptoms, which may all be part of the picture.

To overcome situational depression, what part does treatment play?

The rehabilitation process for situational depression can be significantly aided by therapy, especially cognitive-behavioural therapy (CBT) and supportive counselling. In treatment, people learn to recognize and question negative thought patterns, build coping mechanisms, work through feelings connected to the stressor, and discover ways to deal with stress and problems. Individuals can overcome their challenges and develop resilience in a therapeutic setting.

Is it essential to use medicine to overcome situational depression?

Medication isn't always needed to get over situational depression, mainly if the symptoms aren't too severe and can be managed with therapy and other supportive measures. In extreme circumstances, however, medication may be recommended to help with symptoms and speed up the healing process. A mental health expert should be consulted before making this decision.

How can one recover from situational depression with the help of self-care practices?

Recovering from situational depression relies heavily on self-care activities. You may boost your mood, reduce stress, and promote general well-being by exercising regularly, eating healthily, getting enough sleep, practicing relaxation techniques like deep breathing or meditation, and doing things you like. A regular schedule and reasonable objectives might also aid in the healing process.

When it comes to overcoming situational depression, how might social support play a role?

Social support from friends, family, or support groups is a great asset to validate one's feelings, get practical help, and feel connected to others during recovery. Reducing feelings of loneliness, encouraging one another, and providing perspective on coping with the stressor are all possible outcomes of having a supporting network to rely on. Having social support might also make getting the help you need easier.

How can one tell if they are making headway in their battle against situational depression?

Lessening depressive symptoms, better coping with stresses, enhanced functioning in everyday life, increased participation in social interactions and activities, and optimism or hope for the future are all possible indicators of progress in recovery from situational depression. On the road to recovery, it's crucial to celebrate little wins and recognize progress.

Once a person has overcome situational depression, are there any ways they might avoid relapsing?

Proper coping mechanisms, awareness of recurrence warning signals, support system utilization, and ongoing self-care are all important components of a relapse prevention plan for situational depression. Individuals can learn to cope with depressive episodes and avoid relapse by creating a plan with the support of a therapist or mental health expert. This plan can include identifying triggers for developing resilience and coping mechanisms.

In overcoming situational depression, what part does strengthening one's resilience play?

It is crucial to strengthen one's resilience so that one can recover quickly from setbacks and successfully face difficult situations in the future to overcome situational depression. To become more resilient, one must learn to cope, build support systems, be optimistic, reframe negative beliefs, and find significance in challenging times. A person's capacity to deal with and recover from stress in the long run can be improved by cultivating resilience.

To overcome situational depression, how can one alter their way of life?

Making positive changes to one's lifestyle can aid in the healing process from situational depression by increasing one's resilience and general sense of well-being. Improving mood, reducing depressive symptoms, and increasing coping abilities are all possible outcomes of embracing a healthy lifestyle that incorporates frequent exercise, a nutritious diet, sufficient sleep, and stress management strategies. Another factor that can help with rehabilitation is avoiding substances and making self-care a priority.

In overcoming situational depression, what part does goal-setting play?

Setting goals is an essential part of getting over situational depression because it gives people something to work towards and keeps them motivated. A sense of agency and self-assurance can be restored, and obstacles can be conquered when people set short-term and long-term objectives that are both reasonable and attainable. Setting goals might also help you track your progress and monitor your rehabilitation.

How many practices of relaxation and mindfulness aid in the healing process of situational depression?

Recovering from situational depression can be aided by practicing mindfulness and relaxation techniques. These practices help with self-awareness, emotional regulation, and stress reduction.

Depression symptoms, excessive ruminating, and an imbalanced mind can be better managed with the use of practices like guided imagery, progressive muscle relaxation, deep breathing exercises, and mindfulness meditation. You may improve your health and resilience by making these practices a part of your daily life.

In the process of overcoming situational depression, what part does practicing appreciation play?

Recognizing and appreciating the good things in life might help alleviate situational depression by redirecting one's attention away from bad feelings and thoughts. Individuals can reframe their views and cultivate a sense of serenity and resilience through practicing gratitude, which entails intentionally recognizing and appreciating benefits, minor delights, and acts of kindness. Maintaining an attitude of thankfulness through regular journaling or acts of kindness can help with emotional health and healing.

When getting over situational depression, how can one keep tabs on how they're doing and what changes have occurred?

Recovery from situational depression can be tracked by maintaining a mood or symptom journal, creating personal objectives and milestones, and periodically checking in with yourself about your thoughts, feelings, and behaviors. It can help individuals monitor their progress and identify changes as they work through the process. Gaining insight into one's recovery experience and identifying opportunities for continued growth and development can be achieved through reflecting on improvements, setbacks, and coping techniques. Additional viewpoints on accomplishments and areas of concentration can be gained by seeking comments from trusted individuals or healthcare providers.

When getting over situational depression, what are some of the obstacles that people may encounter?

Setting-backs or relapses, trouble consistently implementing coping mechanisms, lingering impacts of the stressor, social stigma or lack of understanding from others, and feelings of discouragement or hopelessness are some potential obstacles that individuals may encounter while recovering from situational depression. Realizing that obstacles are inevitable on the road to recovery and reaching out for help when required are crucial.

How can people who are suffering from situational depression find and connect with others who can help them get back on their feet?

When recovering, it might be helpful to surround yourself with people who understand what you're going through. It can be friends, family, support groups, or mental health experts. They can offer emotional validation, practical help, and encouragement. Individuals should surround themselves with supportive, understanding, and nonjudgmental people who will not judge them or their needs, and they should actively seek out such influences.

When overcoming situational depression, what methods may people employ to deal with potential stresses and triggers?

It can be helpful to practice relaxation techniques, exercise, seek social support, express emotions creatively (through art or journaling), set boundaries, and solve problems effectively. Individuals can better manage stress and overcome obstacles if they have a toolbox of coping mechanisms and learn good ways to deal with it.

As they work to overcome situational depression, how can people find and maintain a sense of meaning and purpose in their lives?

Finding one's unique set of values, interests, and aspirations is the first step in developing a life with meaning and purpose. Doing good deeds, volunteering, following one's interests, making connections, and giving back to one's community are all examples of what this may entail. Essential parts of the healing process include rediscovering one's identity, rekindling one's motivation, and reestablishing one's optimism for the future.

How might getting help from a mental health expert aid in overcoming situational depression?

Professional support services like counselling, medication management, and mental health care can significantly aid treatment for situational depression. Helping people overcome obstacles, cope with symptoms, and address underlying issues, mental health experts offer evidence-based therapies, individualized interventions, and counselling specific to each person's requirements. Getting help from a trained expert can hasten healing, enhance results, and lessen the likelihood of a recurrence.

After overcoming situational depression, how can one keep their gains and avoid relapsing?

Staying connected with supportive networks, prioritizing self-care practices, monitoring mental health, engaging in ongoing therapy or counseling as needed, and developing a relapse prevention plan with healthcare providers are all ways to maintain progress and prevent relapse after recovering from situational depression. This strategy may involve identifying triggers, early warning indicators, coping mechanisms, and support systems to assist individuals in recognising and handling possible problems before they get worse. Maintaining recovery and promoting long-term well-being can be achieved through regular self-assessment, self-awareness, and proactive stress management.

Chapter Six

How to avoid developing situational depression (an adjustment disorder characterized by a gloomy mood) at the workplace

What are some typical elements that could lead to situational depression in the workplace?

High job demands, low job control, poor interpersonal relationships, bullying or harassment at work, supervisors' lack of support or recognition, work-life imbalance, job insecurity, organizational changes or restructuring, and so on are common workplace factors that can lead to situational depression.

How can stress in the workplace affect mental health and lead to situational depression?

Stress at the workplace can have a detrimental effect on mental health by setting off a chain reaction of events that might lead to or worsen situational depression. Workplace stress increases the likelihood of developing depressive symptoms through its adverse effects on mental health, including feelings of emotional tiredness, burnout, and overwhelm.

When it comes to avoiding workplace situational melancholy, how vital is work-life balance?

It is crucial to have an excellent work-life balance to avoid suffering from situational depression on the job. People can better handle stress, recharge, and participate in things that make them happy when they manage their professional and home lives in a balanced way. Businesses can help employees achieve a better work-life balance by creating an environment prioritising their health and happiness, providing more leeway in scheduling, and encouraging generous vacation plans.

To avoid situational depression, how can people deal with stress at work?

"Mindfulness," "deep breathing exercises," and "progressive muscle relaxation" are all stress-reduction methods that people can use to deal with the stress that comes with their jobs. One way to alleviate emotions of helplessness and overwhelm is to set reasonable goals, set priorities, and divide up work. Additional strategies for reducing job stress include regular exercise, taking breaks, and reaching out to coworkers for social support.

What steps can businesses take to foster a positive work environment for employees' mental health and to reduce the prevalence of situational depression?

The following are ways employers can help foster a mentally healthy workplace: encouraging open communication, making available resources for mental health support, establishing employee assistance programs (EAPs), training managers to identify the symptoms of distress, and enacting policies to alleviate stress in the workplace. To further contribute to employee well-being and minimize situational depression, promoting work-life balance, cultivating an inclusive and supportive culture, and offering chances for professional development and advancement are essential.

How can people in the workplace learn to spot the symptoms of situational depression in themselves or those around them?

By keeping an eye out for shifts in demeanor, conduct, or productivity on the job, individuals can spot the symptoms of situational depression in themselves or those around them. Depression can manifest in a variety of ways; some of these symptoms include a lack of motivation, irritability, social withdrawal, decreased productivity, altered eating or sleeping habits, and trouble focusing. Addressing concerns with empathy and providing support or encouragement to seek help when necessary are crucial.

For employees who are dealing with situational depression, what tools are available on the job?

It's not uncommon for companies to provide wellness programs, counseling services, employee assistance programs (EAPs), and mental health awareness training to help their employees who are going through tough times mentally. Workers can consult with human resources, supervisors, or reliable colleagues for more assistance. People are more likely to seek treatment when they need it if there is a culture of transparency and stigmatization surrounding mental health issues.

How can people in the workplace protect their mental health by setting limits and speaking up when they need help?

Effective communication regarding workload, deadlines, and personal constraints with supervisors and colleagues enables individuals to maintain boundaries and advocate for their mental health needs. An individual's ability to handle stress and avoid situational depression can be enhanced by setting reasonable expectations, making self-care a priority, and asking for help when needed. Respecting the needs of others and meeting the expectations of one's employment requires a certain level of assertiveness.

When it comes to avoiding workplace situational melancholy, how important is social support?

Employees who have social support systems in place are less likely to experience situational depression on the job. These networks give people a feeling of belonging, validate their feelings, and offer practical help when needed. To mitigate the harmful impacts of stress in the workplace and boost resilience, it helps to have helpful coworkers, supervisors, and an overall supportive organizational culture. Establishing a welcoming workplace where everyone feels appreciated and supported by cultivating friendships, encouraging one another, and building solid relationships is possible.

How can people foster an upbeat workplace to lessen the likelihood of situational depression?

By encouraging teamwork, mutual regard, and gratitude, individuals can create a supportive workplace that lowers the risk of situational depression. It is essential to promote cooperation, acknowledge contributions, and celebrate successes to raise morale and foster a sense of camaraderie. A positive work environment, where employees are motivated and engaged, can be achieved through effective communication, the constructive resolution of problems, and empathy towards coworkers.

When avoiding workplace situational melancholy, what part does contentment with one's employment play?

A person's level of job satisfaction affects their general health and happiness, which in turn helps to avoid workplace situational depression. People are less prone to suffer from depression if they are happy with their jobs, tasks, and workplace. Employees' emotional and psychological well-being is enhanced by work-life balance, meaningful work, career advancement possibilities, and leadership that supports them.

To avoid situational depression, how can people deal with workplace perfectionism and unreasonable expectations?

Practicing self-compassion, creating reasonable goals, and organizing one's workload are effective strategies for dealing with workplace perfectionism and unreasonable expectations. Individuals can ease pressure and reduce the likelihood of situational depression by recognizing that mistakes are a natural part of learning and by pursuing progress rather than perfection. A more positive attitude towards work and less likelihood of burnout can be achieved through adopting a growth mindset, actively seeking feedback to improve, and setting realistic goals.

How can people deal with problems at work in a way that doesn't exacerbate their situational depression?

Active listening, seeking understanding, and finding mutually beneficial solutions are strategies for negotiating workplace issues and preventing them from contributing to situational depression. People can learn to handle problems constructively and stop confrontations from worsening by practising assertiveness, effective communication, and conflict resolution techniques. Resolving conflicts and creating a healthy work environment can also be achieved by setting boundaries, managing emotions, and getting advice from supervisors or HR specialists.

How can businesses encourage open dialogue about mental health and remove the stigma associated with employees who need assistance?

By fostering an environment of transparency and inclusivity, educating and training employees on mental health issues, and providing access to counseling and support services, employers may help raise awareness about mental health and reduce the stigma associated with getting help when needed. People are more likely to seek help when they need it, and there are fewer hurdles to treatment when mental health talks are normalized, misconceptions are addressed, and confidential services are made available.

When it comes to reducing situational depression among employees, what role can leadership and organizational support play?

The leadership and support of an organization are crucial in reducing situational depression in the workplace because they establish the norms for behavior, rules, and regulations. Leadership that cares about its employees is open and honest with them, and encourages them to feel like they belong can help establish a psychologically safe workplace. Supporting work-life balance, investing in staff development, and acknowledging the impact of work-related stress are all ways for organizations to show they care about mental health and help with preventative initiatives.

How can people avoid developing situational depression by strengthening their resilience to deal with stress at work?

To become more resilient, one must learn to cope with stress healthily, surround themselves with supportive people, and keep a positive attitude when things get tough. Strengthening one's resilience can be achieved through self-care practices like exercise, mindfulness, and relaxation techniques. Another way to enhance resilience and avoid situational depression is to set attainable objectives, reframe negative beliefs, and look for ways to improve personally.

Regarding avoiding situational melancholy, what part do workplace policies and procedures play?

By reducing exposure to systemic stresses and encouraging a positive work atmosphere, workplace policies and practices can significantly reduce the prevalence of situational depression. Employee health and depression prevention efforts are enhanced by policies that support a healthy work-life balance, allow for some leeway in scheduling, and enable access to mental health services. Workplace mental health and the prevention of depression can be enhanced by implementing equitable performance evaluation criteria, recognizing employees' efforts, and promoting an inclusive and respectful work environment.

How can people avoid situational sadness by using their time well and reducing their workload?

Setting priorities, creating limits, and implementing time management skills are excellent ways to manage workload and time.

One way to avoid feeling overwhelmed and reduce stress is to break work into smaller, more manageable chunks. Another strategy is to delegate responsibility when possible and set reasonable deadlines. People should use productivity tools like calendars or task management applications to stay focused, avoid burnout, and plan for frequent breaks.

How can one recognize if an employee is suffering from situational depression on the job?

Persistent sadness or tearfulness, changes in sleep or appetite, irritability, difficulty concentrating, decreased productivity, withdrawal from social interactions, increased absenteeism, and a general lack of interest in work or activities are all warning signs that an individual may be experiencing situational depression in the workplace. Early recognition of these signals and providing support or resources can aid in preventing symptoms from worsening.

How can people in the workplace help foster an environment where mental health is acknowledged and supported?

People can help foster an environment where mental health is acknowledged and supported by starting conversations, sharing stories or resources, and fighting for policies and programs that address mental health. To destigmatize obtaining treatment for mental health issues, it is essential to actively listen to coworkers, provide support without passing judgment, and maintain confidentiality. Another way to help create a welcoming environment at work is to participate in mental health awareness programmes or training and encourage others to do the same.

Preventing situational depression at school

In what ways might students' daily habits exacerbate the symptoms of situational depression?

The following lifestyle variables might lead to situational depression among students: social pressures, lack of sleep, unhealthy eating habits, inactivity, and insufficient coping mechanisms. Preventing situational depression requires juggling academic and extracurricular obligations, keeping up positive relationships, and taking care of oneself.

How can children deal with the pressures of school without succumbing to depression?

Students can deal with academic pressure by listing everything they need to do, dividing big projects into smaller ones, and asking for help when needed. Other ways to reduce stress and avoid situational sadness include making a regular study plan, setting attainable goals, and learning relaxation techniques.

How can students' social networks help them avoid developing situational depression?

Students are less likely to experience situational depression when they have social support, which can offer them emotional affirmation, company, and practical help. To better manage stress and maintain mental health, it is helpful to surround oneself with supportive friends and family, get involved in extracurricular activities, and talk to trusted adults or a counselor as needed.

How can students avoid developing situational depression by leading healthy lives?

A healthy lifestyle may be maintained by students as long as they make time for regular exercise, eat a balanced diet, and get enough sleep. Promoting general health and resilience to stress can be achieved by regular physical activity, a varied diet rich in nutrients, and a regular sleep schedule. It's crucial to stay away from substances and practice good coping techniques like mindfulness or keeping a journal to avoid situational depression.

How can school personnel and teachers help students who are experiencing situational depression?

A healthy school climate, supportive connections, and mental health support resources are ways that school staff and educators can help reduce the prevalence of situational depression among children. Students might be better equipped to handle difficult situations and avoid depression if they receive instruction on stress management, learn coping mechanisms, and participate in peer support groups.

When it comes to school, how can parents help their children avoid developing situational depression?

Parents can help their children avoid school-related depression by providing a supportive home environment, encouraging open communication, and setting a good example when it comes to coping strategies. It is vital to encourage academic accomplishment without excessive pressure, promote extracurricular activities, and advocate for mental health resources at school to assist children's well-being.

How can teachers and parents recognize if a youngster is suffering from situational depression?

Students may be suffering from situational depression if they exhibit the following symptoms: changes in mood or behavior, isolation from friends and classmates, a drop in grades, disturbed eating or sleeping habits, and an overwhelming sense of worthlessness or despair. Educators and parents should watch for these warning signals so they can step in early to provide support and, if needed, seek professional assistance.

What steps may be taken by schools to foster a caring atmosphere that can help children avoid developing situational depression?

By establishing all-encompassing mental health programs, educating personnel to identify and handle mental health issues, and making counseling services easily accessible, schools may foster an accepting atmosphere that protects pupils from situational depression. Additionally, a supportive school climate must prioritize the promotion of strong peer relationships, the eradication of bullying and harassment, and the cultivation of an inclusive and accepting culture.

To what extent can students' participation in extracurricular activities mitigate the risk of developing situational depression?

Thanks to the chances for social interaction, skill development, and stress release that extracurricular activities provide, they significantly contribute to minimising situational depression among students. Participating in extracurricular activities like athletics, the arts, clubs, or volunteer work can help alleviate academic stress, boost self-esteem, and provide a sense of belonging, which can lower the risk of depression.

How can students avoid feeling overwhelmed or depressed by learning to manage their time wisely?

Creating a study timetable, prioritising work, and dividing assignments into digestible portions can help students efficiently manage their time and avoid feelings of overwhelm and situational depression. Students can improve their organization skills and decrease their tendency to procrastinate using time management tools like planners or digital applications. Limiting screen time and social media usage can also improve time management and mental health.

How can educational institutions lessen the burden of homework and protect students against the onset of situational depression?

By encouraging a growth attitude, providing academic support services, and taking a more balanced approach to education, schools can help alleviate academic pressure and lower the risk of situational depression. Student resilience and stress reduction can be enhanced by implementing project-based learning, integrating mindfulness techniques into the curriculum, and accommodating grading standards.

To avoid developing situational depression, how can students learn to cope healthily?

By teaching themselves stress management skills, doing relaxation exercises, and reaching out to people they trust, students can build healthy coping strategies that will help them avoid situational depression. Students are better equipped to handle difficulties and keep their mental health in check when they learn to persevere in the face of hardship, maintain an optimistic view, and solve problems creatively.

Do students who practice self-care have a lower risk of developing situational depression?

By fostering physical, emotional, and mental wellness, self-care is essential in reducing the prevalence of situational depression among students. Recharging energy stores, reducing stress, and improving resilience are all outcomes of regular exercise, hobbies, creative expression, and relaxing practices.

How can educational institutions raise consciousness about mental health issues and remove the stigma associated with students who may be suffering from situational depression?

The inclusion of mental health education in the curriculum, the provision of counseling services, and the promotion of an accepting and open culture are all ways in which schools may assist in raising awareness about mental health issues and remove the stigma associated with getting help, especially for students dealing with situational depression. It is crucial to normalize conversations about mental health, provide peer support groups, and educate staff to recognize the symptoms of depression to foster a caring school climate.

If a kid is suffering from situational depression or is looking for ways to prevent it at school, what resources are there for them?

School counselors, peer support groups, crisis hotlines, internet resources, mental health programs, and situational depression prevention tactics are some of the school resources that may be accessible to kids. Additional support services and treatment referrals can be provided by schools in collaboration with community organizations or mental health experts. It is vital to treat situational depression effectively by encouraging students to seek help and providing discreet outlets for support.

Chapter Seven

Myths and misconceptions about situational depression (an adjustment disorder characterized by sad mood)

Situational depression is merely a transitory change in mood and not a severe mental illness.

Sadness, pessimism, and a lack of interest or enjoyment in once pleasurable activities are symptoms of situational depression, a real mental health disorder. It may be caused by a particular event or stress in life, but either way, it may make everyday life very difficult and distressing.

Unlike clinical depression, situational depression is not life-threatening and does not necessitate medical attention.

The severity of situational depression and the need for professional treatment are determined by the symptoms and distress level of the individual. It might get better with time without treatment, but in the meantime, you might need medicine, therapy, or something else to help with the symptoms and stop them from worsening.

Situational depression is exclusively experienced by those who are emotionally frail.

People of any age, from any walk of life, and with any personality type can experience situational depression. It is a normal reaction to difficult situations or stresses in life and should not be seen as a sign of weakness. A proactive step towards enhancing mental well-being and coping with challenging emotions is seeking help for situational depression.

People with situational depression don't need help because it's a natural part of being human.

Although it is expected to feel down or distressed when faced with changes or stresses in life, persistent or severe depression could be a sign of a more serious issue. Ignoring or not seeking help for situational depression can make symptoms worse and make it harder to operate every day. Therapy and support groups are examples of interventions that might help people cope and find community.

Attempting to think positively or "snap out of it" can automatically alleviate situational sadness.

It's possible that self-care and optimistic thinking won't be enough to cure situational depression symptoms, but they can help manage them. Treatment for situational depression typically involves medication or therapy to help with coping and getting to the root of the problem.

A significant life event, like a loss or tragedy, is always the catalyst for situational depression.

A single major life event can bring on situational depression, but it can also be the consequence of a cascade of more minor stresses or persistent problems. Furthermore, particular people may have a higher susceptibility to experiencing situational depression as a result of psychological, biological, or genetic causes.

Reacting negatively to a challenging situation is the same as suffering from situational depression.

Although it's normal to feel depressed when faced with adversity, situational depression is characterized by deep and persistent feelings of melancholy, despair, or hopelessness that significantly interfere with daily functioning. It may necessitate the assistance of a medical expert and be accompanied by tangible symptoms like changes in eating or sleep patterns.

Seeking help is unnecessary because situational depression is only a temporary state.

Some people with situational depression may feel better after a while, but others may continue to struggle or even get worse if they don't get help. If you or someone you care about is struggling with situational depression, talking to a mental health expert can assist with validation, support, and treatment options.

People should be able to conquer situational sadness by themselves because outside forces always bring it on.

Situational depression is typically brought on by things beyond one's control, such as stressful life events or financial difficulties. Still, it can also have an internal component, like one's genes, biology, or personality attributes. People with situational depression may also benefit from medication, therapy, or other types of assistance to help them manage their symptoms, so it's essential to seek professional intervention if needed.

People with situational depression can "get over it" if they put in enough effort; it's simply a type of attention-seeking behaviour.

No, situational depression is an actual mental illness that calls for compassion, understanding, and the right kind of help. Neglecting or downplaying another person's difficulties or experiences can make them feel even more alone and hopeless. Advocating for individuals to reach out for assistance and offering empathetic support can significantly enhance their road to recovery.

Adolescents and younger children are not vulnerable to situational depression; it only affects adults.

Young people, like adults, are not immune to the effects of situational depression. A variety of stresses, including academic pressure, family disputes, social difficulties, or traumatic experiences, can lead to situational depression in young people. It is crucial to identify and treat mental health issues in youth to avoid long-term effects.

People should be able to tackle their issues independently; situational despair is a sign of weakness or failure.

"Situational depression" is an actual mental illness that can strike anyone; it has nothing to do with a person's inherent frailty or lack of success. As a proactive measure towards self-care and wellness, seeking treatment for situational depression is a good thing to do. Realizing you have problems and asking for help shows strength and resilience.

People should stay away from those who are depressed if they want to avoid getting depressed themselves.

"Situational depression is not contagious," so people shouldn't be afraid to talk to someone who's going through it. On the contrary, providing someone with compassion, empathy, and support can significantly assist them in managing situational depression. Healing and recovery can be aided by fostering open conversation and offering a safe environment for expression without judgment.

People with situational depression will never fully recover and will constantly face challenges related to it.

With the right help, many people with situational depression can overcome their symptoms and get back on their feet. Effective symptom management and improved quality of life can be achieved through the use of medication, counselling, behavioral modifications, and coping mechanisms. People can learn to deal with life's difficulties and become more resilient with the correct help and therapy.

People with situational depression should not seek professional care right away because it is merely a brief mood disturbance, contrary to popular belief.

Although specific stresses or life events might set off situational depression, it's essential to get treatment for this condition because it can lead to a lot of problems if ignored. If you are struggling with situational depression, it may be helpful to seek the advice of a mental health professional who can offer you support, direction, and treatment options. If symptoms are caught early on, they have a better chance of not worsening and recovering faster.

People should be able to overcome situational despair by simply using their willpower.

Anyone can experience situational despair; it does not reflect your character. Determination might not be enough to beat depression on its own. People can get the assistance and resources they need to manage their symptoms and improve their health by seeking professional aid, including medication or therapy.

People with situational depression can eventually overcome it on their own. Intervention is unnecessary.

Without treatment, situational depression can get worse or stay the same, even though it gets better for some people with time. There may be long-term effects and difficulties with everyday functioning if depressed people ignore their symptoms and do not seek treatment. People suffering from depression might find relief and get to the root of their problems by consulting a mental health expert.

Feeling down or depressed because of a problematic situation is the same as situational depression, and treatment is unnecessary for this type of depression.

Situational depression is characterized by acute and persistent emotions of melancholy, hopelessness, or despair that disrupt daily functioning. Feeling sad or down in reaction to a challenging situation is natural, but these feelings must not be recurrent or severe. Medication or therapy may be required to improve general health and reduce symptoms.

People with situational depression can't help but want attention; they can "snap out of it" if they put in the effort.

Situational depression is a complicated mental illness that requires more than just "trying harder." Constructing an attention-seeking person out of someone else's experiences or invalidating their experiences can make them feel even more alone and ashamed. It would be more helpful to offer empathy, understanding, and encouragement to get expert help.

A particular event always triggers situational depression, and the depression will go away after the event is over.

Although specific stresses or life events can set off situational depression, it doesn't mean that once the event is over, the depression will go away. Some people's symptoms could linger long after the initial cause has gone. Essential parts of treatment include learning appropriate coping techniques and addressing underlying issues.

About the   Author

ADEGBOYE S. ADURAGBEMI is an African manager, business administrator, entrepreneur, and motivational speaker. ADEGBOYE has a BA from Yale University, an IPMA from Adonai University, and a Master's in Business Administration (MBA) from the University of Salford, Manchester.

He was born in South Africa but is presently based in Nigeria as a motivational speaker and marriage counselor in institutions, sectors, and seminars with young and upcoming managers all over Africa.

Acknowledgements

I want to express my sincere gratitude to everyone who helped with the "FAQ on Communication in Marriage." Their encouragement, insight, and support have been priceless throughout this journey.

I want to start by acknowledging the fact that, without God, this guide wouldn't have been possibly achieved.

And also, to my spouse, who has always been motivating and supportive in making this task successful, I will always love and appreciate you.

I have many couples to appreciate who have shared their experiences, challenges, and victories with me over the years. Your openness, weakness, and tenacity have enhanced the book's pages and provided priceless insights into the difficulties of marriage communication.

My sincere gratitude goes to my family and friends for their continuous support and encouragement during this journey. Your wise advice, tolerance, and words of support have helped me get through the complicated process of writing and releasing this book.

I sincerely thank the specialists and experts who kindly offered their knowledge and skills in marriage and communication. Your advice and thoughts have improved this book's quality and depth, and I appreciate your contributions. Finally, I would like to express my profound gratitude to all of the readers of this work. As you journey through the communication process in your marriage, I hope that the knowledge, direction, and encouragement provided within these pages will inspire and empower you. I sincerely appreciate your help.

Printed in the USA
CPSIA information can be obtained
at www.ICGtesting.com
CBHW062005021124
16780CB00072B/982